A BRIEF HISTORY OF PANICS

A BRIEF HISTORY OF PANICS

AND THEIR PERIODICAL OCCURRENCE
IN THE UNITED STATES

BY

CLEMENT JUGLAR

MEMBER OF THE INSTITUTE, VICE-PRESIDENT OF LA SOCIÉTÉ
D'ÉCONOMIE POLITIQUE

THIRD EDITION
TRANSLATED AND EDITED WITH AN INTRODUCTION AND
BROUGHT DOWN FROM 1889 TO DATE

BY

DeCOURCY W. THOM

FORMER MEMBER OF THE BALTIMORE STOCK EXCHANGE AND OF THE
CONSOLIDATED EXCHANGE OF NEW YORK

REPRINTS OF ECONOMIC CLASSICS

AUGUSTUS M. KELLEY · PUBLISHERS

First edition 1893
Third edition 1916
(New York: G.P. Putnam's Sons, 1916)

Reprinted 1989 by
AUGUSTUS M. KELLEY, PUBLISHERS
Fairfield NJ 07006-0008

Library of Congress Cataloging-in-Publication Data

Juglar, Clément, 1819-1905.
A brief history of panics and their periodical
occurrence in the United States.

(Reprints of economic classics)
Translation of: Des crises commerciales.
Includes index.
1. Business cycles—United States—History.
2. United States—Economic conditions. I. Thom,
DeCourcy W. (DeCourcy Wright), 1858-1932.
II. Title. III. Series
HB3743.J8513 1989   338.5'42   87-17069
ISBN 0-678-00168-5

Manufactured in the United States of America

TO GOLDEN DAYS

Tonight at "Blakeford," I set down this dedication of the third edition of this book which has proved to be the pleasant companion of two visitations—one at "Wakefield Manor," Rappahannock County, Virginia, in 1891, the other at my old home "Blakeford," Queen Anne's County, Maryland, in 1915. The memories that entwine it there and here mingle in perfect keeping and have made of a dry study something that stirs anew within me as I consider the work accomplished, my love and remembrance of the old days, and my love and unforgettingness of these other golden days under whose spell I have brought the book up to the present year.

DeCourcy W. Thom.

"Blakeford,"
October 10, 1915.

PREFACE TO THIRD EDITION

THE second edition of this study of *Panics in the United States* brought us through the year 1891. I originated about one fourth of it.

This third edition brings us practically up to date. Of this edition I originated about one half. I hope it will prove helpful in many ways. I trust that it will force an appreciable number of men to realize that "business" or "financial" panic is not merely fear, as some have asserted; but is based upon the knowledge that constriction, oppression, unhappy and radical change in this, that, or the other kind of business must tend to drag down many others successively, just as a whole line of bricks standing on end and a few inches apart will fall if an end one is toppled upon its next neighbor. Indeed, the major cause of "business" or "financial" panic is just reasoning upon existing conditions rather than a foolish fear of them. Over-trading and loss of nerve constitute the medium. Recent national legislation has gone far in enabling the business world in the United States to prevent panics, and farther yet in providing the means to cope with them when, in spite of precautions, they shall recur.

DeC. W. Thom.

"Blakeford,"
October 10, 1915.

A BRIEF HISTORY OF PANICS

INTRODUCTION

COMPRISING A CONDENSATION OF THE THEORY
OF PANICS, BY M. JUGLAR, RENDERED INTO
ENGLISH, WITH CERTAIN ADDITIONAL MA-
TERIAL, BY DeCOURCEY W. THOM.

IN this translation, made with the
author's consent, my chief object being to
convey his entire meaning, I have unhesi-
tatingly rendered the French very freely
sometimes, and again very literally. Style
has thus suffered for the sake of clear-
ness and brevity, necessary to secure
and retain the attention of readers of this
class of books. This same conciseness has
also been imposed on our author by the in-
herent dryness and minuteness of his faithful inquiry into hundreds of figures, tables
showing the condition of banks at the time
of various panics, etc., etc., essential to his
demonstration. As an extreme instance of
the latitude I have sometimes allowed my-

1

self, I cite my rendering of the title: "*Des Crises Commerciales et de Leur Retour Periodique en France, en Angleterre et aux États-Unis*" merely as "Panics and Their Periodical Occurrence in the United States": for M. Juglar himself states that a commercial panic is always a financial panic, as a falling away of the metallic reserve indicates its breaking out; and I have only translated that portion dealing with the United States, deeming the rest unnecessary, for this amply illustrates and proves the theorem in hand.

To this sketch of the financial history of the United States up to 1889, when M. Juglar published his second edition, I have added a brief account to date, including the panic of 1890, the table headed "National Banks of the United States," and some additions to the other tables scattered through this book.

From the prefaces to the French editions of 1860 and of 1889, and other introductory matter, I have condensed his theory as follows:

A Crisis or Panic may be defined as a

stoppage or the rise of prices: that is to say, the period when new buyers are not to be found. It is always accompanied by a reactionary movement in prices.

A panic may be broadly stated as due to overtrading, which causes general business to need more than the available capital, thus producing general lack of credit. Its precipitating causes are broadly anything leading to overtrading:

In the United States they may be classed as follows:

1. **Panics of Circulation,** as in 1857, when the steadily increased circulation, which had almost doubled in nine years, had rendered it very easy to grant excessive discounts and loans, which had thus overstimulated business so that the above relapse occurred; or, we may imagine the converse case, leading to a quicker and even greater disaster: a sudden and proportionate shrinkage of circulation, which, of course, would have fatally cut down loans and discounts, and so precipitated general ruin.

2. A Panic of Credit, as in 1866, when the failure of Overend, Gurney, & Co. rendered the whole business world over cautious, and led to a universal shrinkage of credit. [I take the liberty of adding that it seems evident to me that such a danger must soon confront us in the United States, unless our Silver Law is changed, because of a finally inevitable distrust of the government's ability to keep 67-cent silver dollars on an equality with 100-cent gold dollars.]

3. Panics of Capital, as in 1847, when capital was so locked up in internal improvements as to prove largely useless.

4. General Tariff Changes. To the three causes given above the translator adds a fourth and most important one: Any change in our tariff laws general enough to rise to the dignity of a new tariff has with one exception in our history precipitated a panic. This exception is the tariff of 1846, which was for revenue only, and introduced after long notice and upon a graduated scale. This had put the nation at large in such good condition that when the apparently inevitable Decennial Panic occurred in 1848 recovery from it was very speedy.

The reason for this general effect of new tariffs is obvious. Usual prices and confidence are so disturbed that buyers either hold off, keeping their money available, or else draw unusually large amounts so as to buy stock before adverse tariff changes, thus tightening money in both ways by interfering with its accustomed circulation. This tendency towards contraction spreads and induces further withdrawal of deposits, thus requiring the banks to reduce their loans; and so runs on and on to increasing discomfort and uneasiness until panic is speedily produced. The practical coincidence and significance of our tariff changes and panics is shown by an extract below from an article written by the translator in October–November, 1890, predicting the recent panic which was hastened somewhat by the Baring collapse.[1]

[1] *Inter-relations of Tariffs, Panics, and the Condition of Agriculture, as Developed in the History of the United States of America.*

This brief sketch of our economic history in the United States seeks to show that Protective Tariffs have always im-

The retarding or precipitating influence of a good or bad condition of agriculture upon the advent of a panic is also indicated.

poverished a majority of our people, the Agriculturists ; that agriculture has thus been made a most unprofitable vocation throughout the States, and that this unsoundness at the very foundation of the business of the American people has often forced our finances into such makeshift conditions, that under any unusual financial strain a panic, with all its wretched accompaniments, has resulted.

To consider this properly, we must note the well known fact that in this land, those who live by agriculture directly, are more than one half of our population. Their votes can cause to be made such laws as they see fit, hence, one would expect the enactment of laws to raise the price of farm products, and to lower the price of all that the farmer has to buy. But the farmers vote as the manufacturers and other active classes of the minority of our voters may influence ; and only twice in our history, from 1789 to 1808, and from 1846 to 1860, have enough of the minority found their interests sufficiently identical with that of the unorganized farmer-majority to join votes, and thus secure at once their common end. In consequence of this coalition during these two periods, two remarkable things happened : 1st, agriculture flourished, and comfortable living was more widely spread : 2d, panics were very infrequent, and the hardships and far-reaching discomforts that must ever attend adjustments to new financial conditions after disturbances were, of course, minimized.

It is not fair to deduce very much from the first period of prosperity among the farmers, 1789 to 1808, for, during this time, there were no important business interests unconnected with agriculture ; but we may summarize the facts that from 1789 to 1808, there was, 1st, no protection, the average duty during this time being 5 per cent., and that laid for revenue only ; 2d, that agriculture flourished ; 3d, that there was not a single panic.

The symptoms of approaching panic, generally patent to every one, are wonderful prosperity as indicated by very numer-

"The Embargo" of 1808, followed by the Non-Intercourse Act in 1809 and the War of 1812-15, and the war tariff, by which double duties were charged in order to raise money for war purposes, caused us to suffer all the economic disasters flowing from tariffs ranging between absolute protection, and those practically prohibiting, and intensified by the sufferings inseparable from war.

During this period agriculture, for the first time in our history, was in a miserable condition. It is significant that for the first time too, we had a protective tariff. Though our people made heroic efforts to make for themselves those articles formerly imported, thus starting our manufacturing interests, they had, of course, lost their export trade and its profits. When the peace of 1814 came, we again began exporting our produce, and aided by the short harvests abroad, and our own accumulated crops, resumed the profitable business which for six years our farmers and our people generally had entirely lost.

Our first panic, that of 1814, came as a result of our long exclusion from foreign markets, being followed by the stimulation given business through resumption of our foreign trade in 1814, which was immensely heightened by the banks issuing enormous quantities of irredeemable paper, instead of bending all their energies to paying off the paper they had issued during the war.

But worse than the suffering entailed by this panic, was the engrafting upon our economic policy of the fallacious theory made possible by the Embargo and the Non-Intercourse Act, (which was equivalent, let me enforce it once more, to that highest protective tariff, a prohibitory one) that *all infant manufactures must be protected, that is, guaranteed a home market*, though such home market be one where all goods cost more to the purchaser than similar goods bought elsewhere,

ous enterprises and schemes of all sorts,
by a rise in the price of all commodities,
of land, of houses, etc., etc., by an active

and this in order that the compact little band of sellers in the
home market may make their profit. This demand for protection was made by those who had started manufactures during the years from 1808 to the end of the war of 1815, when,
as we have seen, imports were practically excluded.

In 1816 their demand met explicit assent, for, in the tariff of
that year, duty for protection, not for revenue, was granted ;
and an average of 25 per cent. duties for six years, to be followed by an average of 20 per cent. duties, was laid upon
imports. For a few years bad bread crops in Europe, demand
for our cotton, and an inflation of our currency delayed a
panic.

But, we had started on our unreasoning course. We had
tried to ignore the laws of demand and supply, and had for-
gotten that it is also artificial to attempt preventing purchases
in the cheapest, and selling in the highest markets ; and to
help a few manufacturers we had put up prices for all that a
large majority of our population,—the agriculturists mainly—
had to buy. In a short while the demand for what the
farmers had to sell fell away, and bills could not be met, and
their troubles were added to those of the minority of the con-
sumers of the country ; the volume of business fell off, and a
panic came in 1818. The influences that led up to it continued until 1846, as follows : The great factors in producing
this state of affairs were the successive tariffs of 1818, with
its 25 per cent. duty upon cottons and woollens, and its increased duties on all forms of manufactured iron, (the tariff of
1824 which increased duties considerably), and the tariff of
1828, imposing an average of 50 per cent. duties, and in which
the protective movement reached its acme (omitting, of course,
the present McKinley Bill with its 60 per cent. average duty).
In 1832, consequently, a great reaction in sentiment took

request for workmen, a rise in salaries, a
lowering of interest, by the gullibility of
the public, by a general taste for specu-
lating in order to grow rich at once, by a
growing luxury leading to excessive expenditures, a very large amount of discounts
and loans and bank notes[1] and a very small

---

place, and the " Compromise Tariff " was passed and duties
were lowered. From this period, the advocacy of a high
tariff in order to protect " Infant Industries," no longer "Infant" was largely abandoned, and its advocacy was generally
based upon the fallacy, less obvious then than now, of secur-
ing high wages to laborers by means of high import duties.
This plea for high duties the laborer found to be fallacious.

They (agriculturists mainly) found that they had to pay
more for manufactured goods, so that the manufacturers
could still buy their raw materials at the advanced prices, pay
themselves the accustomed or increased profits, and then
possibly pay the laborer a small advance in wages.

The advance did not compensate for increased cost of necessaries of life. If competition reduced the manufacturers'
profit, the first reduction of expenses was always in the
laborer's pay. The recognition of these truths brought about
the further reduction of duties until 1842, in which year the
tariff was once more raised. It was not until 1846 that we
enjoyed a tariff which sought to eliminate the protective
features. It is significant that a period of greater profit and
stability among our business men, but especially among our

---

[1] Our recent banking history has proved rather an exception to this law as far as bank notes are concerned, because of
the obviously unusual cause of sudden and enormous calling
in of government bonds, the basis of bank-note issue.

reserve in specie and legal-tender notes and
poor and decreasing deposits.

On the other hand, the lowest point of
___

farmers, was then inaugurated.   This was the first tariff, since
that of 1816, not affected by politics.   It lasted until 1857,
and the country flourished marvellously under it.

From 1816, when protection was first resorted to, until to-
day, tariff rates have been almost continually raised, mainly
by votes of the agriculturists, misled by the manufacturers and
politicians, influenced by the manufacturers' money.   And a
fact worth noting is that financial panics have come quick
and furious.   They came in 1818, and in 1825–26, in 1829–30,
and so on, (see page 13).   Sudden changes in our tariff rates
have unvaryingly been followed by financial panics within a
short period.   Changes to lower rates have not brought panics
so quickly as changes in the reverse direction.

Low tariff without protective features, maintained steadily,
has been coincident with constantly increasing prosperity to
the country at large : but most especially to the agriculturists.
This is readily understood, for purchases of imported and manufactured goods and all outfit needed for the farmers' land
and family can be made at low—and owing to the competition
that always arises to supply a steady and natural market—lowering prices.   Moreover, the settled prices prevailing throughout the country allow of assured calculations and precautions
as to business ventures, and permit such a ratio to be established between expenses and income, that at the end of the
fiscal year a profit, not a loss, may be counted upon.

This was the experience of our agriculturists during the
second and last prosperous time of our farmers, 1846–60.
During that period agriculture flourished ; the tariff was low
and there were only two panics, that of 1848, and the one of
1857, and the first (a non-protective one) should not be considered as precipitated by the tariff of 1846, except that some
few suffered briefly in readjusting themselves to the changed,

depression following a panic is accompanied by the converse of the symptoms just enumerated.

(though better),condition of the new tariff. The vast majority of the nation reaped enormous benefits from the changes inaugurated.

The panic of 1857 was caused by over-activity in trade speculation, and over-banking, and the tariff of the same year was really passed to help avert the panic threatening. It had the contrary effect, it is believed, for it still further, of course, unsettled rates for goods, when prices were already unstable. But the point is to be noted that in reality tariff change followed practical panic in this instance rather than practical panic tariff change. The high protective war tariffs, beginning in 1860, and increased for war purposes and granted largely as an offset for those internal revenue taxes laid to carry on the war, have been continued as a body ever since, as is well known, despite the internal revenue taxes having been abolished except on whiskey and tobacco. It is equally well known that farming has grown less and less remunerative since 1860, and that the panics of 1864, 1873, and 1884 have been unfortunate culminations of almost unceasing financial discomfort, which has been most forcibly exemplified during the last two months. Even now the financial fabric is in unstable equilibrium, and this latest monstrosity—the McKinley Bill—imposing the highest tariff we have ever exacted—an average duty of 60 per cent., and coming when a panic was due, bids fair to hurry us into another and a terrible financial panic. If it does not do so, it will be because our crops are too bountiful to allow it, but it will at least have made the agriculturists and all buyers of other commodities than agricultural produce pay more for all purchases. It will bring no more money into their pockets, but it must take out considerably more. The people appreciate this. The nation's pocket nerve has been touched. This is the meaning

Bank balance sheets reflect in cold figures the result of the above influences. Prices being high, and discounts and loans

of the recent election, it seems to the writer. But whether the impending danger can be averted even if a prompt, though wise and slow reversal of tariff policy can be forced by the next Congress is doubtful, for unrest and timidity have been evoked and require time to be allayed before easy and orderly business operations will in general be resumed, unless indeed bountiful crops here and demand abroad once again reverse the logic of the situation.

Certain it is that our tariff laws must interfere as little as possible with the natural law of demand and supply in making prices, or we must be content to suffer from the instability that artificiality always brings with it.

Our plain duty is to enact as speedily as possible a tariff that shall by small but continued changes cut down our protective duties and substitute non-protective duties until our tariff is for revenue only ; for thus and thus only can the vast majority of the agriculturists buy what they need most cheaply, and so find that to purchase necessaries does not cost them more than the total of their sales ; and our exports of produce, chiefly owing to agricultural prosperity, would increase, thus materially helping to build up our general business so that the other nations will have to pay us, in the gold we require for comfortable management of our business, the growing trade balances against them.

The rough table below suggests that sudden tariff changes have precipitated panics, which have come quickly if the change was to higher protective duties and somewhat slower if the change was to lower protective duties ; that slow and well considered changes doing away with protective duties generally have not caused disturbances ; and that agriculture has flourished in proportion as we approached tariff for revenue only. It has for obvious reasons required about one year for

large in proportion to deposits, and having steadily increased for years, danger
is near ; further, when discounts and loans

---

financial trouble to be shown by decrease in value of farm
produce as evinced by wheat-flour exports.

Special conditions, such as excessive wheat corps here and
deficiency abroad or special tariff favors to flour export, may
even increase the amount exported despite an otherwise untoward effect of the new tariff upon farmers. I have selected
flour exports as the article best reflecting the chief interest of
the farmers, and at the same time the state of general business
for manufacturing, transportation and such other branches as
are concerned with it.

TAR-IFFS.	They have all been de-signedly Pro-tective save the one of 1846.	Panics.	Condition of agriculture and incidentally of general business as suggested by export of wheat-flour from 1790–1890.		
			Year.	Barrels.	Dollars.
			1790..	724,623	4,591,293
			1791..	619,681	3,408,246
			1792..	824,464	....
			1793..	1,074,639	....
			1794..	846,010	....
			1795..	687,369	....
			1796..	725,194	....
			1797..	515,633	....
			1798..	567,558	....
			1799..	519,265	....
			1800..	653,056	....
			1801..	1,102,444	....
			1802..	1,156,248	....
			1803..	1,311,853	9,310,000
			1804..	810,008	7,100,000
			1805..	777,513	8,325,000
			1806..	782,724	6,867,000

are not only large in proportion to deposits, having increased steadily for years, and then suddenly fallen off noticeably for a

			1807..1,249,819	10,753,000
			1808.. 263,813	1,936,000
			1809.. 846,247	5,944,000
			1810.. 798,431	6,846,000
			1811..1,445,012	14,662,000
Say 1814	Practical exclusion of all imports through the war = Prohibitory Tariff.	1814	1812..1,443,492	13,687,000
			1813..1,260,943	13,591,000
			1814.. 193,274	1,734,000
			1815.. 862,739	7,209,000
1816	Duties for six years @ 25% and thereafter @ 20%.		1816.. 729,053	7,712,000
			1817..1,479,198	17,751,376
		1818	1818..1,157,697	11,576,970
			1819.. 750,669	6,005,280
			1820..1,177,036	5,296,664
1818	Duties 25% on Cotton and Woollens, and all duties on Manufactured Iron increased.		1821..1,056,119	4,298,043
			1822.. 827,865	5,103,280
			1823.. 756,702	4,962,373
		1825–26	1824.. 996,792	5,759,176
			1825.. 813,906	4,212,127
			1826.. 857,820	4,121,466
			1827.. 868,492	4,420,081
1828	Average duty of 50%.		1828.. 860,809	4,286,939
			1829.. 837,385	5,793,651
			1830..1,227,434	6,085,953
			1831..1,806,529	9,938,458
			1832.. 864,919	4,880,623
1833	Compromise Tariff, gradual reduction of duties from 50% average until in 1842 the average was 20%. But this was levied for Protection not merely for Revenue.	1836–39	1833.. 955,768	5,613,010
			1834.. 835,352	4,520,781
			1835.. 779,396	4,394,777
			1836.. 505,400	3,572,599
			1837.. 318,719	2,987,269
			1838.. 448,161	3,603,299
			1839.. 923,151	6,925,170
			1840..1,897,501	10,143,615
			1841..1,515,817	7,759,646
1842	Imposed higher duties.		1842..1,283,602	7,375,356
			1843.. 841,474	3,763,073
			1844..1,438,574	6,759,488
			1845..1,195,230	5,398,593

considerable time, only to increase again, danger is imminent.

On the other hand, a steady and radical

1846 Imposed lower duties and these were not for Protection purposes they were simply for Revenue.	**1848**	1846..2,289,476	11,668,669
		1847..4,382,496	26,133,811
		1848..2,119,393	13,194,109
		1849..2,108,013	11,280,582
		1850..1,385,448	7,098,570
		1851..2,202,335	10,524,331
		1852..2,799,339	11,869,143
		1853..2,920,918	14,783,394
		1854..4,022,386	27,701,444
		1855..1,204,540	10,896,908
		1856..3,510.626	29,275,148
1857 Reduced Tariff rates on above plan because of redundant prosperity.	**1857**	1857..3,712,653	25,882,316
		1858..3,512,169	19,328,884
		1859..2,431,824	14,433,591
1860 War Tariff protection restored as compensation for Internal Revenue taxes.	**1864**	1860..2,611,596	15,448,507
		1861..4,323,756	24,645,849
1862..As above..........		1862..4,882,033	27,534,677
1864..As above..........		1863..4,390,055	28,366,069
		1864..3,557,347	25,588,249
		1865..2,641,298	27,507,084
		1866..2,183,050	18,396,686
		1867..1,300,106	12,803,775
		1868..2,076,423	20,887,798
		1869..2,431,873	18,813,865
		1870..3,463,333	21,169,593
		1871..3,653,841	24,093,184
1872 10% reduction, but coffee and tea put on Free List and whiskey and tobacco taxes reduced.	**1873**	1872..2,514,535	17,955,684
		1873..2,562,086	19,381,664
		1874..4,094,094	29,258,094
		1875..3,973,128	23,712,440
		1876..3,935,512	24,433,470
1875 10% reduction above repealed.		1877..3,343,665	21,663,947
		1878..3,947,333	25,095,721
		1879..5,629,714	29,567,713
		1880..6,011,419	35,333,197
		1881..7,945,786	45,047,257
		1882..5,915,686	36,375,055

reduction of loans and discounts, following
a panic and extending until new enterprises are very scarce, till prices are very
low, till there is wide-spread idleness
among workmen, a decrease in salaries and
in interest rates, when the public is wary
and speculation dead, and expenditures
are cut down as far as possible, may be
taken to mean a rapid and continued resumption of every prosperous business : but
if the above process is only partially performed, renewed trouble must result;—in
other words, liquidation to really be helpful
(to congested business) must be thorough.

A study of the first of the following
tables, " National Banks of the United
States," illustrates the above generaliza-
tion. It is unnecessary to mention that
1873, 1884, and 1890 have been the

1883 { Duties really raised on class of goods most used, but apparently lowered the tariff, for it considerably reduced rates on many little used classes of goods. }	1884	1883..9,205,664 54,824,459 1884..9,152,260 51,139,695 1885.10,648,145 52,146,336 1886..8,179,241 38,442,955 1887.11,518,449 51,950,082 1888.11,963,574 54,777,710 1889..9,374,803 45,296,485
1890 { McKinley Bill average of 60% duty. }	1890	1890.12,231,711 57,036,168 1891.11,344,304 54,705,616

		1892 . . 15,196,769	75,362,283
1893–4	Free silver and sudden ill-distributed and drastic tariff reductions and insufficient revenue.	1893 . . 16,620,339	75,494,347
		1894 . . 16,859,533	69,271,770
		1895 . . 15,268,892	51,651,928
		1896 . . 14,620,864	52,025,217
1897		1897 . . 14,569,545	55,914,347
		1898 . . 15,349,943	69,263,718
		1899 . . 18,485,690	73,093,870
		1900 . . 18,699,194	67,760,886
		1901 . . 18,650,979	69,459,296
		1902 . . 17,759,203	65,661,974
1903	Tariff disturbance to higher rates. The propaganda for keener regulation of business.	1903 . . 19,716,484	73,756,404
		1904 . . 16,699,432	68,894,836
		1905 . . 8,826,335	40,176,136
		1906 . . 13,919,048	59,106,869
1907		1907 . . 15,584,667	62,175,397
		1908 . . 13,937,247	64,170,508
		1909 . . 10,521,161	51,157,366
		1910 . . 9,040,987	47,621,467
		1911 . . 10,129,435	49,386,946
		1912 . . 11,006,487	50,999,797
1913	Tariff reductions to produce a revenue; not on a protective basis. The further regulating of business. The "World War."	1913 . . 11,394,805	53,171,537
		1914 . . 12,768,073	62,391,503

TABLE NO. 1.—NATIONAL BANKS OF THE UNITED STATES.

YEAR	MONTH	LOANS AND DISCOUNTS	"WORKING CAPITAL."				Excess of Capital (Surplus, plus Undivided Profits) over Loans and Deposits and Discounts	Percentage "Working Capital" exceeds Loans and Discounts	Difference between Deposits and Loans and Discounts	Percentage of Difference (over or under) between Deposits and Loans and Discounts
			Capital	Undivided Profits and Surplus, etc.	Deposits	TOTAL				
		5.000 to 10.000 Millions	7.000 to 14.740 Millions	0.000 to 0.330 Millions	8.097 to 19.080 Millions	15.818 to 34.000 Millions	10.847 to 23.000 Millions		3.031 Millions	
1863	Oct. 5	166	135	20	183	338	152	65.4	+ 17	35 over
1864	Jany. 4	500	493	71	522	996	496	69.2	+ 22	45 over
1865	Jany. 2	608	420	86	558	1064	456	47.7	+ 50	9
1866	Jany. 1	616	420	101	534	1055	439	49.8	+ 85	4
1867	Jany. 7	644	419	116	568	1103	459	44.8	— 76	8 under
1868	Jany. 6	688	426	124	546	1096	408	41.6	— 148	15
1869	Jany. 4	767	444	140	561	1145	378	37.2	— 206	13
1870	Jany. 22	839	464	147	593	1204	365	33.	— 247	20
1871	Mch. 18	913	484	163	656	1303	390	30.3	— 357	36
1872	Feby. 27	897	490	173	647	1258	361	30.2	— 308	41
*1873	Feby. 28	956	496	182	620	1325	369	28.6	— 309	29
1874	Feby. 27	950	504	184	659	1308	358	27.8	— 330	52
1875	Mch. 1	920	493	167	602	1319	399	27.3	— 261	47
1876	Mch. 10	854	473	165	643	1240	386	30.2	— 252	53
1877	Jany. 20	823	462	153	848	1258	399	31.1	— 186	39
1878	Mch. 15	974	454	159	933	1461	435	34.5	— 126	40
1879	Jany. 1	1073	458	176	1036	1567	487	33.3	— 140	44
1880	Feby. 21	1182	469	191	1004	1696	494	31.5	— 146	27
1881	Mch. 11	1249	490	196	1046	1770	514	30.3	— 245	14
1882	Mch. 11	1321	515	209	1046	1726	441	26.1	— 275	15
1883	Mch. 13	1367	524	206	1152	1897	449	25.3	— 236	14
*1884	Mch. 7	1515	533	212	996	1726	494	28.6	— 215	24
1885	Mch. 10	1584	555	231	1224	2079	494	27.9	— 201	26
1886	Mch. 1	1724	582	246	1251	2219	530	24.6	— 333	23
1887	Mch. 4	1844	596	269	1334	2395	495	23.7	— 237	18
1888	Feby. 14	1927	626	290	1479	2461	515	23.1	— 365	23
1889	Feby. 26	2044	662	316	1483	2711	551	22.2	— 444	26
*1890	Feby. 28		679	330	1702		534	21.7	— 342	35
1891	Feby. 26						567	24.6		24
1892	Mch. 1									20

NOTE.—These figures are for the standing at the first part of the year as indicated.

* Panic Years.

TABLE NO. 1.—NATIONAL BANKS OF THE UNITED STATES.—*Continued.*

YEAR	MONTH	LOANS AND DISCOUNTS.	"WORKING CAPITAL." Capital.	"WORKING CAPITAL." Undivided Profits and Surplus, etc.	"WORKING CAPITAL." Deposits.	"WORKING CAPITAL." Total.	Excess of Capital (Surplus, Undivided Profits, plus Deposits) over Loans and Discounts.	Percentage "Working Capital" exceeds Loans and Discounts.	Difference between Deposits and Loans and Discounts.	Percentage of Difference (over or under) between Deposits and Loans and Discounts.
		Millions	In Millions.			Millions	Millions		Millions	
1893	Mch. 6	2159	688	348	1751	2787	627	22.6	—408	23.3 under
1894	Feby. 28	1872	678	332	1586	2596	724	27.9	—286	18.8
1895	Mch. 5	1965	662	329	1667	2658	693	26.2	—298	17.8
1896	Feby. 28	1966	653	334	1648	2635	669	25.4	—318	19.2
1897	Mch. 9	1808	642	333	1669	2644	746	29.	—229	13.6
1898	Feby. 18	2152	628	334	1982	2944	792	27.6	—170	8.5
1899	Feby. 4	2299	608	303	2082	3172	873	28.3	—67	3.
1900	Feby. 13	2481	613	363	2481	3457	976	25.7	+61	0.
1901	Feby. 5	2814	634	398	2753	3785	971	23.7	—146	2.2
1902	Feby. 25	3128	607	448	2382	4097	969	24.	—191	4.9
1903	Feby. 6	3350	731	516	3159	4406	1056	25.1	—169	5.6
1904	Jany. 22	3469	765	562	3300	4627	1158	25.1	—116	5.1
1905	Jany. 11	3728	776	580	3612	4977	1279	26.5	—17	3.2
1906	Jany. 29	4071	814	589	4088	5537	1466	21.3	+17	.41 over
1907	Jany. 26	4463	860	635	4115	5664	1201	23.2	—348	8.4 under
1908	Feby. 14	4422	905	689	4105	5752	1330	24.4	—317	7.7
1909	Feby. 5	4840	927	742	4699	6398	1558	25.	—141	2.9
1910	Jany. 31	5229	960	778	5190	6968	1739	22.9	—39	.73
1911	Jany. 7	5402	1007	884	5113	7004	1602	23.5	—289	5.6
1912	Feby. 20	5810	1031	927	5630	7588	1778	23.4	—180	3.1
1913	Feby. 4	6125	1048	958	5985	7991	1866	23.0	—140	2.3
1914	Jany. 13	6175	1057	991	6072	8120	1945	23.0	—103	1.7
1915	Mch. 4	6499	1066	1012	7148	9226	2727	20.6	+649	9.9 over

TABLE No. 2.

United States Table of Balance Sheets.

MILLIONS OF DOLLARS.

YEAR	CIRCU-LA-TION	SPECIE ON HAND	DIS-COUNTS AND LOANS	INDI-VIDUAL DEPOSITS	NUMBER OF BANKS	CAPITAL
1811	28	15			89	52
1815 *	45	17			208	88
1816 *	68	19			246	89
1819	35	9	73			72
1820 *	44	19		35	308	137
1830	61	22	200	55	330	145
1834	94					
1835	103	43	324	75	506	200
1836	140	40	365	83 / 115	704	231
1837	149	37	457	127	713	251
1838	116	35	525 / 485	84	788	290 / 317
1839 *	135	45	492	90	829 / 840	327
1840	106	33	462	75	901	358
1841	107	34	386	64	784	313
1842	83	28	323	62	692	260
1843	58	33	254	56	691	228
1844	75	49	264	84	696	210
1845	89	44	288	88	707	206
1846	105	42	312	96	707	196
1847	105	35	310	91	715	203
1848 *	128	46	344	103	751	204
1849	114	43	332	91	782	207
1850	131	45	364	109	824	217
1851	155	48	413	128	879	227
1854	204	59	557	188	1208	301
1855	186	53	576	190	1307	332
1856	195	59	634	212	1398	343
1857 *	214	58	684	230	1416	370
1858	155	74	583	185	1422	394
1859	193	104	657	259	1476	401
1860	207	83	691	253	1562	421
1861	202	87	696	257	1601	429
1862	183	102	646	296	1492	418
1863 *	238	101	648	393	1466	405

* PANIC YEARS

TABLE No. 3.

UNITED STATES TABLE OF BALANCE SHEETS OF THE NATIONAL BANKS—QUARTERLY STATEMENT.

MILLIONS OF DOLLARS.

YEAR	CIRCU-LA-TION		SPECIE ON HAND		LEGAL TENDERS		DIS-COUNTS AND LOANS		INDI-VIDUAL DEPOSITS		NUMBER OF BANKS		CAPITAL		SURPLUS AND UNDIVIDED PROFITS	
	MAX.	MIN.	MAX.	MIN.	MAX.	MIN.	MAX.	MIN.	MAX.	MIN.	MAX.	MIN.	MAX.	MIN.	MAX.	MIN.
1865	66			4	72		166		183		1500		393		20	
2ND QUAR																
3RD "			18		189											
4TH "	171						487									
1866																
2ND "	213		19		187		500		500							
3RD "											522	1644	415		71	
4TH "	280															
1867				9	205		603		564							
2ND "									558							
3RD "											512	1642	420		86	
4TH "	293					92										
1868			20		114		609		532		1643		420		101	
2ND "						84										
3RD "																
4TH "	295															
1869			29				657		580		1617		426		116	
2ND "						80										
3RD "																
4TH "			48													
1870							686		574							
2ND "							688				511	1648	430		124	
3RD "			18		94	79			546							
4TH "	296								501							
1871							725									
2ND "					122	93										
3RD "			13								1790		458		140	
4TH "	318				97											
1872							831		611							
2ND "					122											
3RD "			10								1940		479		147	
4TH "	336								620							
1873 *			16		10	97	885		656							
2ND "	339															
3RD "			19						622		616	1976	491		163	
4TH "	341		33			92	944									
1874					103											
2ND "			21					856	540		595	2027	493		173	
3RD "						80	897		602							
4TH "		331					955		695							
1875			8				994									
2ND "											2087	504			182	
3RD "									618							
4TH "		314				7										

* PANIC YEARS

MILLIONS OF DOLLARS.

YEAR	CIRCULATION MAX. MIN.	SPECIE ON HAND MAX. MIN.	LEGAL TENDERS MAX. MIN.	DISCOUNTS AND LOANS MAX. MIN.	INDIVIDUAL DEPOSITS MAX. MIN.	NUMBER OF BANKS MAX. MIN.	CAPITAL MAX. MIN.	SURPLUS AND UNDIVIDED PROFITS MAX. MIN.
1876 2nd QUAR.		21			612	2,089	499	184
3rd "								
4th "	291 32		90					
1877	290	49	66	929	659	2080	479	
2nd "								
3rd "		21						
4th "			66					167
1878		54		881	604	2053	466	165
2nd "		29			625			
3rd "								
4th "	303							
1879		41	64	826	588	2048	454	153
2nd "				814				
3rd "								
4th "	321	79	54	933	765			
1880		86						
2nd "		109	105	974		2090	457	159
3rd "	317		64	1040				
4th "								
1881	298 128		52	1000	933	2132	463	
2nd "								176
3rd "								
4th "	323							
1882		112 109		1100	1100 1000	2268	483	
2nd "		102	68	1200	1122			191
3rd "								
4th "	315							
1883		304 115 97			1000	2501	509	196
2nd "								
3rd "								
4th "								
1884 *		109 128 167	80 75 77	1300 1308 1200	1100 1000 875	2664	524	209
2nd "	288							
3rd "								
4th "								
1885	248	177 171	79 69		1100	2714	527	206
2nd "								
3rd "								
4th "			62					
1886	202	171 149		1470	1152 1172	2852	548	212
2nd "								
3rd "								
4th "								
1887	164	171	79 73	1587	1285	3049	578	231
2nd "		159						
3rd "								
4th "								
1888	151 182	178 172	83			3120	588	246
2nd "								
3rd "								
4th "								
1889	126		81 97	1684	1356	3170	596	269
2nd "		164						
3rd "								
4th "								
1890 *	123	171 178 190	84	1811	1436	3383	626	290
2nd "								
3rd "								
4th "								
1891	123	199	82	1832	1331 1575 1525	493 3601	662	316
2nd "								
3rd "			100					
4th "								
1892 †	341 230		99	1962 2044	742	3711	679	330

* PANIC YEARS
† FIRST QUARTER ONLY

TABLE No. 5 (*No. 3 continued*).
MILLIONS OF DOLLARS.

YEAR	CIRCULATION	SPECIE ON HAND	LEGAL TENDERS	DISCOUNTS AND LOANS	INDIVIDUAL DEPOSITS	NUMBER OF BANKS	CAPITAL	SURPLUS AND UNDIVIDED PROFITS
	MAX. MIN.	MAX. MIN.	MAX. MIN.	MAX. MIN.	MAX. MIN.	MAX. MIN.	MAX. MIN.	MAX. MIN.
1892								
2ND QUAR		239			1765			
3RD "			113	2171				
4TH "	145	209				3784	689	353
1893								
1ST "	149		90	2161	1751	3830	688	352
2ND "		186						
3RD "	182	251	131	1843				
4TH "					1451			
1894								
1ST "	174	259	146		1872	3777	678	
2ND "		169		2007	1728			
3RD "			119					
4TH "		218						339
1895								
1ST "		169 220			1965	3728	662	
2ND "								
3RD "					1736			
4TH "	185	196	93	2059				340
1896								
1ST "		187		1982	1687	3699	653	
2ND "		196	118					
3RD "								
4TH "	210		110	1893	1597			342
1897								
1ST "	202	233						
2ND "			126			1669 3634	642	
3RD "								
4TH "	193	252	107	2100	1916			341
1898								
1ST "	184	271	120			3594	628	
2ND "								
3RD "								
4TH "			110	2214	2225			340
1899								
1ST "		371	116				608	
2ND "	199							
3RD "								
4TH "		314	101	2496	2522	3602		363
1900								
1ST "	204	339	122					
2ND "								
3RD "								
4TH "			145	2706	2623	3942	632	403
1901								
1ST "	309	399						
2ND "								
3RD "		369	164					
4TH "			151	3038	2964	4291	665	448
1902								
1ST "	309							
2ND "	309		164					
3RD "								
4TH .."		366	141	3303	3209	4666	714	516
1903								
1ST "	335							
2ND "			163		3200			
3RD "								
4TH "		378	142	3481		5118	758	564

MILLIONS OF DOLLARS.

YEAR	CIRCU-LA-TION		SPECIE ON HAND		LEGAL TENDERS		DIS-COUNTS AND LOANS		INDI-VIDUAL DEPOSITS		NUMBER OF BANKS		CAPITAL		SURPLUS AND UNDIVIDED PROFITS	
	MAX.	MIN.	MAX.	MIN.	MAX.	MIN.	MAX.	MIN.	MAX.	MIN.	MAX.	MIN.	MAX.	MIN.	MAX.	MIN.
1904																
1ST QUAR.	380			453												
2ND "					169											
3RD "			504				3772		3707		5477		776		594	
4TH "																
1905																
1ST "	424				178											
2ND "			495			157										
3RD "				460			4016		3889		5833		808		632	
4TH "																
1906																
1ST "	498	492			175											
2ND "																
3RD "				459												
4TH "						152	4366		4289		6199		847		687	
1907																
1ST "					173											
2ND "	543															
3RD "																
4TH "			531			151	4678		4319		6625		901		749	
1908																
1ST "																
2ND "					192											
3RD "																
4TH "	599		680				4840		4720		6865		921		779	
1909																
1ST "					198											
2ND "	615															
3RD "																
4TH "			694			176	5148		5120		7006		953		825	
1910																
1ST "	667															
2ND "																
3RD "																
4TH "			672			169	5467		5304		7204		1004		894	
1911																
1ST "	680				168											
2ND "																
3RD "			761		185											
4TH "							5663		5536		7328		1026		930	
1912																
1ST "	704				188											
2ND "			769													
3RD "																
4TH "							6058		5944		7420		1046		969	
1913																
1ST "	717	749			189											
2ND "																
3RD "																
4TH "							6260		6051		7509		1059		1007	
1914																
1ST "	720		792		201		6357		6111		7493		1057		1003	
2ND "	1018			746												
3RD "		848		534		128					7581		1065		1007	
4TH "																
1915																
1ST "		746		591		127	6499		6348		7599		1066		1012	

last three panic years. But it is very necessary in studying this table, to bear in mind that its figures are taken from the standing of the banks at the first of the year, while the panics generally occurred later in the year: the last two, for instance in the second and fourth quarter, respectively. The third and fourth tables will give more exact figures in this connection. Table Two, dealing with State Banks, is given merely to round out our banking history as told in figures.

The increase or diminution of deposits of course reflects a confident and successful, or a panicky and impoverishing, state of general business.

The adage "buy cheap and sell dear," or its practical equivalent—so scary and imitative are investors—*Buy during the last of a selling movement and sell during the last of a buying movement,* resolves itself, we venture to repeat, into: *Buy when the decline caused by a panic has produced such liquidation that discounts and loans, after steady and long-continued diminution, either become stationary for a period,*

*or else increase progressively coincident
with a steady increase in available funds;
and sell for converse reasons.*

These conclusions are also reached by
our author through analyses of the Financial History of England, France, Prussia,
Austria, etc. These I omit as unnecessarily
wearisome to the reader since I give that
of our own country. However, I will here
quote the following: " What must be noted
is the reiteration and sequence of the same
points *(faits)* under varying circumstances,
at all times, in all countries and under all
governments," and also this table showing
all the panics and their practical coincidence
in the past eighty-five years, in

France	England	and the United States.
1804	1803	
1810	1810	
1813–14	1815	1814
1818	1818	1818
1825	1825	1826
1830	1830	1829–31
1836–39	1836–39	1837–39
1847	1847	1848
1857	1857	1857
1864	1864–66	1864
	1873	1873
1882	1882	1884
1889–90	1890–91	1890–91
1894	1894	1893–94
1897	1897	1897
1903	1903	1903
1907	1907	1907
1913	1913	1913
(approximately)	(approximately)	

Truly these thirteen panics in the three countries have been practically simultaneous and one common cause must have originated them. The only cause common to all was overtrading to such an extent that neither credit nor money were to be had, so that a forced liquidation or panic inevitably ensued.

The above table effectually does away with the theory that new tariffs are directly productive of panics. For most certainly new tariffs did not occur in England, France, and the United States just before or during all the panic years enumerated, and yet, practically simultaneously in free-trade England, high-protection France, and sometimes low-tariff, sometimes high-protection United States have panics occurred for eighty years.

But, as I have shown in a note attached to this Introduction, a new tariff or a general change of duties is apt to precipitate a panic, on account of the unsettling of business, and that the consequent shaking of credit adds its quota to the forces finally culminating in a panic cannot be doubted. As a matter of history with us, substan-

tially new tariffs have always happened to
be the immediate forerunners of a panic,
and this I believe to be true in the case of
other countries.

Why is this? Is it not because the people instinctively turn to tinkering at and
changing their chief tax—the tariff—when·
ever they as a whole need financial relief;
and have we not shown that such relief is
needed almost every ten years, when the
overtrading, inseparable from the development of all thriving communities has made
the call for credit impossible to grant?

A new tariff may defer, or hurry, or,
occurring simultaneously, will intensify a
panic, but it may not hope to avert one
when due: yet if its changes be very grad-
ual, fixed and long predicted, and of a nature
to bring about or confirm a judicious tariff
for revenue only, they will materially help
to put business on so firm and sound a
basis that recovery from the inevitable, and
approximately decennial panics, will be
wonderfully expedited. Thus a new tariff
is a quite accurate forewarning of a panic,
and is also to no inconsiderable extent a

contributory cause. (See foot-note on page 5, *seq., Interrelations of Panics, Tariffs, and the Condition of Agriculture,* etc.; and especially what is said of the panic of 1848, on page 10.)

M. Juglar has fully analyzed the three phases of our business life into Prosperity, Panic, and Liquidation, which three constitute themselves into the business cycle, that for forty years past (that is, since the present Bank of England Act, and practically since that of the Law governing the Bank of France, both of which then increased the required specie reserve) has been of about ten years. These ten years may be apportioned roughly as follows: say, Prosperity for five to seven years; Panic a few months to a few years,[1] and Liquidation about a few years.

I have already pointed out the signs of prosperity, of panic, and of liquidation, but in view of existing conditions perhaps it

---

[1] The panic after 1873 is the only one I know extending to anything like the length it attained. This may be ascribed to the immense development and consequent speculation, and to the inflation of the currency coming after the period about the Civil War.

may be well to restate here the quite familiar fact that the completion of liquidation that precedes the beginning of another period of prosperity is characterized by lack of business, steady prices, and a marked growth in available banking funds.

[The various tables spread through this pamphlet are fully explained by their headings and the text.]

In conclusion I wish to express my thanks for the courtesy M. Juglar has extended me, and to state my appreciation of the motives, painstaking patience, and undoubted originality he has shown in explaining and executing so faithfully and with such genius a most laborious and yet spirited work. It is only justice that such an achievement should have been awarded a prize by the French Institute (Academy of Moral and Political Sciences) and have gained for M. Juglar the Vice-Presidency of the "Society for the Study of Political Economy."

DeCourcy W. Thom.

Wakefield Manor.

A HISTORY OF PANICS IN THE UNITED STATES CONSIDERED WITH SPECIAL REFERENCE TO AMERICAN BANKS.

THE English Colonies soon after their settlement issued paper money. The first was Massachusetts, which issued it even before her independence, in 1690, to obtain funds in order to besiege Quebec.

This example was followed to such an extent that it caused a marked speculation in favor of hard money, varying according to the quantity of notes in circulation. In 1745, after a successful campaign against Louisburg and the taking of that fortress, two million pounds of paper money were issued, which step decreased its value. When liquidation occurred these paper pounds were not worth 10 per cent. of their face value.

The War of Independence obliged Congress to issue three million of paper dollars.

This amount increased to $160,000,000, so that Congress declared, in 1779, that it would not issue more than $200,000,000. Notwithstanding this guaranty, notwithstanding the forced and legal rating conferred by this enactment, notwithstanding the war spirit, it depreciated; and in 1779 it was necessary to decree that, disregarding its normal value, it should be taken at its face. In 1780 it was no longer taken for customs dues. In 1781 it had no rating and was not even taken at 1 per cent. of its face value.

Between 1776 and 1780 the issue of paper money increased to $359,000,000.

Bank of North America.—In 1781 Mr. Morris, Treasurer, persuaded Congress to form a bank (the Bank of North America) with a capital of $10,000,000, of which $400,000 should be turned over to help the national finances. The capital was too insignificant and the course of politics too unpropitious to accomplish this end. However, the example encouraged the States to take up their paper money. Upon the adoption of the United States Constitution

the issuing of paper money ceased, and
gold and silver were the only means of
circulation. Thence arose great embarrassment for the Bank of North America,
which, hampered by its loans to the Gover-
ment, increased its note circulation to an
enormous proportion. The ebb of paper
through every channel finally aroused the
public fears, and people refused the notes.
Every one struggled to obtain metallic
money, hence it became impossible to borrow, and bankruptcy followed. Such was
the excitement that the Philadelphians as
a body demanded and obtained from the
Assembly of Representatives a withdrawal
of the charter; but the Bank, relying
upon Congress, continued until March 17,
1787; succeeded even in extending its
charter fourteen years; and later obtained
a second extension, limited, however, to
Pennsylvania.

The difficulty experienced in the manufacture of money led Mr. Hamilton, Secretary of the Treasury, to propose to Congress in 1790 the founding of a National
Bank. After some doubts as to the power

of Congress, it was authorized. It began operations in 1794, under the title of "Bank of the United States," with a capital of ten millions, eight millions being subscribed by private individuals, and two millions by the Government. Two millions of the first sum were to be paid in metallic money, and six millions in 6 per cent. State bonds; the charter was to run till March 4, 1811. It seemed to be a good thing for the public and the stockholders, for during twenty-one years it paid an average of 8 per cent. dividends. In 1819 the question of renewing its privileges came up, the situation being as follows:

ASSETS.	LIABILITIES.
6 per cent. Paper....$ 2,230,000	Capital Stock....$10,000,000
Loans and Discounts. 15,000,000	Deposits..... 8,500,000
Cash....... 10,000,000	Circulation... 4,500,000

The profits from the Bank, the prosperous state of the country, and the increase of productions led people to think that the issuing of paper money caused it all; seduced by this alluring theory the

"Farmers' Bank" was founded in Lancaster in 1810, with a capital of $300,000. Others followed; such was the mania that the Pennsylvania Legislature was forced to forbid every corporation to issue notes. Despite this preventive message the excitement rose so high that companies, formed to build harbors and canals, also put notes into circulation; in this way the law was eluded.

From 1782 to 1812 the capital of the banks rose to $77,258,000; upon the 1st of January, 1811, there were already eighty-eight banks in existence. Until the declaration of war (June, 1812),the issuing of notes was always made with the intention of redeeming them, but the over-issue soon became general, and depreciation followed. The periodical demands for dollar-pieces for the East Indian and Chinese trade were warnings of the over-speculations on the part of those companies whose members were not personally liable. Traders, who through their notes or their deposits had a right to credit with the banks, did not hesitate to ask for $100,000, where-

as, formerly they would have hesitated to
ask for $1,000.   The war put a stop to the
exportation of precious metals, which, in
the ordinary course of things, limits the
issue and circulation of paper.   The upshot
of this was to redouble the note issue,
each one believing its only duty was to get
the largest amount into circulation.   Loans,
and enormous sums of money, were distributed above all reason among individuals
and among the States.   The increase of
dividends and the ease of obtaining them
extended the spirit of speculation in certain
districts, and especially among those who
owned land. The remarkable results shown
by the Bank of Lancaster, the "Farmers'
Bank," which,by means of an extraordinary
issue of notes, had yielded as much as 12
per cent. and piled up in capital twice the
amount of its stock, caused it to be no
longer thought of as a bank intended to
assist trade with available capital, but as a
mint destined to coin money for all owning
nothing at all.   Led by this error, laborers,
shopkeepers, manufacturers, and merchants
betook themselves to quitting active oc-

cupations to indulge in golden dreams. Fear alone restrained some stockholders connected with the non-authorized companies, and led them to seek for a legal incorporation.

In Pennsylvania, during the session of 1812, an act was passed authorizing twenty-five banks, with a capital of $9,000,000. The Executive nevertheless refused to ratify it, and returned it with some very well-deserved comments. In a second debate the first resolution was rescinded by a vote of 40 to 38. In the following session the proposition was renewed with more vigor, and forty-one banks with a capital of $17,000,000 were authorized by a large majority; the representations of the Executive proved useless, and they immediately entered upon their duties with an insufficient capital.

To discount their own stock was a soon-discovered method. They thus increased the amount of notes, which depreciated in comparison with hard money, and dissipated on all hands the hope of exchanging with it.

In the absence of a demand from abroad for hard money, the demand came from within our own borders.

The laws of New England, which were very severe upon the banks, had placed a penalty of 12 per cent. upon the annual interest payments of those persons who did not pay their notes. The natural result was a difference of value between New England and Pennsylvania, which measured the depreciation caused by paper in the latter district. As remittances on New England could only be made in hard money, the equilibrium of the banks was disturbed; they were not able to respond to the demands for redemption, and a suspension of payments by the banks of the United States, except those of New England, took place in August and September, 1814.

The Panic of 1814.—An agreement took place at Philadelphia between the bank and the chief houses allied with it to resume payments at the end of the war.

Unhappily, the public did not demand the accomplishment of this promise at the time fixed, and the banks, led on by the thirst of gain, issued an unprecedented amount of bank notes. The general approbation brought about a still further increase in their number: the bank notes of the Bank of Philadelphia were at a discount of 80 per cent.; the others at 75 per cent. and 50 per cent., and metallic money disappeared to such an extent that paper had to be used to replace copper coin. The depreciation of fiat money raised the price of everything; this superficial occurrence was looked upon as a real increase, and gave rise to all the consequences that a general inflation of value could produce. This mistake on the subject of artificial wealth made landed proprietors desire unusual proceeds. The villager, deceived by a demand surpassing his ordinary profits, extended his credit and filled his stores with the highest-priced goods; and importations, having no other proportion to the real needs than the wishes of the retailers, soon glutted the market. Every one wished to speculate, and every one eagerly ran up debts. Such was the abundance of paper money that the banks were alarmed lest they could not always find an investment for what they manufactured. It thus happened that it was proposed to lend money on collateral, while the greatest efforts to bring about its redemption were being made. This state of things lasted till the end of 1815, when it was recognized that the paper circulation had not enriched the community, but that metallic money had enhanced.

The intelligent portion of the nation comprehended that even where the estimated value of property had been highest, the true welfare of society had diminished. They learned too late the baleful effects of this circulation of paper money; the greater part of the States and cities had nothing to show for it.

A new class of speculators then appeared, trying to pass these worthless bank notes: forgers of paper money became more active. In the midst of this disorder a National Bank, which should afford a solid basis for the paper circulation, was considered. Influenced by these difficulties, and in hopes of remedying them, the

Secretary of the Treasury proposed to Congress, in September, 1814, a few days after suspension, to found a national bank, in order to re-establish metallic circulation, an end which the State banks had failed to accomplish.

This project, which lent the national credit to the capital of the bank, was antagonized by a good many members who exaggerated its consequences; at the same time that they took more or less important sums in bank notes, or borrowed from the banks upon the nation's guaranty, in order to re-establish the public credit and to obtain means for prolonging the war.

Causes of the Panic of 1814.—The bank directors laid the blame upon the blockade of the ports, which, interfering with, indeed even preventing, the export of products, occasioned the outflow of the metals. The national loans to carry on the war also had their influence. From the beginning of hostilities until 1814 they increased to $52,848,000, distributed as follows: Eastern States, $13,920,000; New York, Pennsylvania, Maryland, and District of Columbia,

$27,792,000 ; Southern and Western States, $11,136,000.

Nearly all of this was advanced by the cities of New York, Philadelphia, and Baltimore. The banks made advances beyond their resources, augmenting their circulation in consequence.[1]

From the 1st of January, 1811, to the 1st of January, 1815, one hundred and

---

[1] The cause of the crisis, according to the Committee of the Senate, was the abuse of the banking system ; the great number and bad administration of the banks ; and their speculations designed to advance their stock, and to distribute usurious dividends. When the Bank of the United States saw the danger that menaced it, it reduced its discounts and circulation. The circulation of the country banks fell from $5,000,-000 to $1,300,000, and the total circulation from $10,000,000 to $3,000,000.

Increase and Decrease Circulation in Pennsylvania.

	City Banks.	Country.	Total.
1814.........	$3,300,000	$1,900,000	$5,200,000
1815.........	4,800,000	5,300,000	10,100,000
1816.........	3,400,000	4,700,000	8,100,000
1817.........	2,300,000	3,800,000	6,100,000
1818.........	1,900,000	3,000,000	4,900,000
1819.........	1,600,000	1,300,000	2,900,000

	Number of Banks.	Capital.	Circulation.	Specie.
1811........	88	$52,000 00	$28,000 00	$15,000 00
1815........	208	82,000 00	45,000 00	17,000 00
1816........	246	89,000 00	68,000 00	19,000 00

twenty new banks were registered, thus
raising their capital to more than $80,000,-
000; this increase took place during a war
that entirely did away with foreign trade.
The expenses of the war declared against
Great Britain in June, 1812, were defrayed
by notes issued by the banks of the various
States. Six million dollars were obtained
from them in 1812, in the following year,
1813, twenty million, and then fifteen million in exchange for twelve million of
Federal stock, issued at the price of $125
face for every $100 paid in. Until Janu-
ary 1, 1814, in order to avoid taxation,
Treasury bonds were issued in addition to
what was contributed by the banks.

In 1812.....................$3,000,000
" 1813..................... 6,000,000
" 1814..................... 8,000,000

Up to this time no account of their
administration had been rendered, but now
Mr. Bland, a Maryland representative,
called attention to the fact that all their
operations seemed veiled from the public.
Unfortunately we have been unable to find
a statement of the discounts.

The suspension of specie payments differed with the corresponding state of affairs in England, inasmuch as it was not general, and, since each State was independent, the depreciation varied. It became very difficult to circulate paper, and the Government was again obliged to issue Treasury bonds, bearing 6 per cent. interest. In February, 1815, peace having been proclaimed, it was hoped that the banks would resume specie payments. There was no sign of it. The re-establishment of peace merely made some of the legal regulations seem less pressing upon the banks.

In the middle of May, 1815, the first English vessel arrived, and business became very active again. In May, June, and July it might have been said "This is the golden age of commerce." Discounts of unsecured paper were easy, and it was not an unusual occurrence to have notes of $60,000 offered.

The banks had authorized a suspension of specie payment in order to force the issue of bank notes, and to stimulate trade, although Mr. Carey pretends that no overtrading had taken place. He blames them

for having restricted their loans in October
and November, thus producing a decline in
prices; and the necessity of cutting down
credits came about, according to him, from
the speculations in National securities.

Six Philadelphia banks with a capital of
$10,000,000 held $3,000,000 in Government stock.

On the 15th of February, 1815, when
scarcely through with all this confusion, an
effort was made to re-establish for the second
time a United States Bank.   It was authorized on the 10th of April, 1816, the Act
permitting the formation of a Company,
with a capital of $35,000,000, divided into
350,000 shares of $100 each, of which the
Government took 70,000 shares and the
public 180,000 shares.   These last were
payable in $7,000,000 of gold or silver, of
the United States of North America, and
$21,000,000 in like money, or, in the funded
debt of the United States either in the 6
per cent. Consolidated Debt at par, the 3
per cent. at 65, or the 7 per cent. at 106½
per cent.; upon subscription $30 was pay-
able, of which at least $5 had to be in gold

or silver; in six months after, $35, of which $10 had to be in metal, and twelve months after the same amount was to be paid in the same manner. The directors were authorized to sell shares every year to the amount of $2,000,000, after having offered them at the current price to the Secretary of the Treasury for fourteen days. The Government reserved the right to redeem the debt at the subscription price.

The charter, made out in the name of the president, ran until March 3, 1836. There were twenty-five directors of the concern, five of whom were appointed by the President of the United States with the consent of the Senate, and not more than three by the State; the stockholders chose the others.

The corporation could not accept any inconvertible property, or any farm-mortgage, unless for its immediate use, either as security for an existing debt, or to wipe out a credit.

It had no right to contract any debt greater than $35,000,000, more than its deposits, unless by special act; the directors were made responsible for every violation, and could be sued by each creditor. They could only deal in gold and silver exchange, and not in other country securities which could not be realized upon at once. The Bank could purchase no public debt nor exceed 6 per cent. interest on its discounts and loans. It could lend no more than $500,000, to the United States, $50,000, to each State, and nothing to foreigners. It could give no bill of exchange greater than $5,000; bank notes less than $100 were to be payable on demand, and greater sums were not allowed to run longer than sixty days. Two settlements were to take place every year.

Branches were to be established upon demand of legislative authorities, wherever 2,000 shares of stock were subscribed for.

There were to be no bank notes less than $5.00, and every bill of exchange, or bill payable at sight, was to be receivable by the public Treasury.

The duty of the Bank was especially to pay out and receive the public money, without profit or loss. It was to serve as agent for every State contracting a loan; the cash belonging to the United States was to be deposited at the Bank whenever the Secretary of the Treasury did not dispose of it otherwise, in which case he was to notify Congress.

Neither the Directory nor Congress could suspend payment of the bank notes, discounts, or deposits: such refusal carried a right to 12 per cent. interest.   In exchange for this charter the Bank was to give $1,000,000, to the Government in three instalments.

The charter was exclusive during its life, excepting in the District of Columbia, where banks might be authorized, provided their capital did not exceed $6,000,000.

The Bank did not open at once, for it sent an agent to Europe to look up bullion. Between July, 1817, and December, 1818, it thus procured $7,311,750, at an expense of $525,000.   On the 20th of February, 1817, it was decided that, excepting gold and silver and Treasury notes, no notes would be received at the Government Treasuries, save such as were payable to the banks in hard money. Notwithstanding this discrimination the banks decided not to resume specie payment until the 1st of July, 1817.

In the meantime an immense speculation had taken place in its stock, which was compromising for the Bank and for the credit of its Directory, because several of its Directors appointed by the Government took part in it. For example, it became customary to loan a very large amount of money on the Bank's own stock, as much as $125 on each share of $100. Thus more than the purchase price was loaned upon them : in furnishing the means of paying for them by credit, speculation was aroused, and on the 1st of September, 1817, the market price advanced to $156.50, at which rate it continued until December, 1818, when it fell to $110.

At last the public perceived that the excessive issue depreciated the bank-note circulation, and that a greater shrinkage was imminent.

An office for the payment of bank dividends was opened in Europe, so as to increase the price of the stock and the speculation in it through this facility, rather than for the permanent benefit of the institution. Let us note here the short-sightedness of the Directors, who thought they would stem the depreciation of their means of payment by persuading all the banks to declare what was not true, that the bank notes were worth par.

On the 21st of February, still aiming at the same end, they announced the resumption of specie payment. The State Banks, remembering the embarrassment of the public, which for two years had paid an exchange of 6 per cent., persuaded themselves that few people would dare to ask for large sums. They hoped to come to an understanding and to cause the acceptance of a promise to pay upon a designated day.

We say "a promise to pay," for this was not a serious proposition, inasmuch as foreign money and that of the United States had enjoyed a higher market value for a long time.

The depreciation of the bank notes might result just as well, from the fear of the public's enforcing its rights, as from a refusal of the banks to make good their promises. This understanding was not, properly speaking, a resumption of specie payment, but rather a kind of humbug.

In January the banks of New York, Philadelphia, Baltimore, Richmond, and Norfolk decided to resume specie payment on the 20th of February, provided the balance showing against them was not demanded by the Bank of the United States before discounts became $2,000,000, at New York, as much in Philadelphia, and $1,500,000 in Baltimore; and these conditions were accepted.

The discount line of the Bank of the United States was thus greatly increased; it grew from $3,000,000 on the 27th of February to $20,000,000 on the 30th of April; to $25,000,000 on July 29th, and to $33,000,000 on the 31st of October. The Bank imported much metallic money, redeemed its notes and those of its branches without distinction; the notes of its Eastern and Southern branches were returned as soon as those of the North had paid them, and they were newly issued; consequently eighteen months after this practice began the cash boxes of the North were drained of their capital, the length of discount was reduced, and 5 per cent. was charged for sixty days. On April 1, 1819, only $126,000, cash remained on hand, on the 12th only $71,000, remained, $196,000, was owed to the city banks.

Scarcely had the Directors of the National Bank succeeded in replacing the paper issued but not redeemed by their bank-note circulation, being fully aware from their own experience that the circulation could only reach a limited amount, than they inundated the market with it, and in a few months all reductions vanished. In this way the market price shortly resumed its former quotation, and all the difficulties reappeared. This imprudent management necessarily threw one portion of the public into debt, from which it had saved itself; and the other portion into the vortex which it had avoided. The critical moment was delayed somewhat, but the day of reckoning was near.

The Panic of 1818.—The Bank at last discovered that it had passed the bounds of safety through its issues, and that it was at the mercy of its creditors. It saw firstly, on October 21, 1818, the payment of part of the State of Louisiana's foreign debt withdraw large sums, and then Chinese, Indian, and other goods reach fancy prices because of the depreciation of the circulating medium. All these influences produced a demand for specie payment which the Bank as a public one was obliged to meet, under penalty of 12 per cent. interest, and without power to avail itself of the same accounts as the State banks.

From this moment it thought fixedly of its safety and of how to reduce its notes; this reduction obliged the other banks to imitate it, and a new crisis shook trade in the end of October, 1818. During one year the National Bank furnished from its cash boxes more than $7,000,000, and the others more than $3,000,000.

The State banks naturally followed the same policy in their connection, and their circulation became reduced as follows:

On November 1, 1816, to............$4,756,000
   "   "   " 1817, " 3,782,000
   "   "   " 1818, " 3,011,000
   "   "   " 1819, " 1,318,000

It will give a faint idea of the excessive issue to state that the only difficulty was the impossibility of examination by the President and Cashier, and of their jointly signing the notes, which was made obligatory by the regulations; hence they asked power from Congress to grant this right to the Presidents and Cashiers of the Branch Banks. This facility was refused, but Congress granted a Vice-President and a Vice-Cashier to sign. With these issues and a simple capital of $2,000,000, the Bank discounted as much as $43,000,000, during one year, in addition to $11,000,000, to $12,000,000, loaned upon public securities.

In order to carry on its operations, it exchanged in Europe a portion of its funded debt for gold and silver, and bought specie in the West Indies. From July, 1817, to July, 1818, it imported $6,000,000, of specie, at an expense of $500,000, but the excessive issue of paper drained away the cash more rapidly than the Bank could import it. In the face of this hopeless struggle, in July, 1818, it entirely changed its course and reduced its discounts, and 10 per cent. premium was then paid for cash, and the reduction of nearly $5,000,000, in the discount line in three months only had a disastrous effect, while at the same time they would only receive for redemption the notes issued by each Branch Bank: hence general embarrassment arose, and as the Bank of the United States was withdrawing cash from the local banks, Congress wished to forbid the exportation of gold and silver. The committee appointed on the 30th of November, 1818, to examine the affairs of the Bank concluded that it had violated its charter:

1. In buying $2,000,000, of the Public Debt.

2. In not requiring from the purchasers of its stock the payment of the second and third instalments in cash, and in the Public Debt of the United States.

3. In paying dividends to purchasers of its stock who had not entirely paid up.

4. In allowing voting by proxy to a greater extent than the charter permitted.

Upon receipt of the report the Governor fled, and the shares fell to $93. In 1818 the speculation was so wild that no one failed on account of a smaller sum than $100,000. A drawing-room that had cost $40,000, and a bankrupt's wine-cellar estimated to have cost $7,000, were cited as instances of the general prodigality.

The Senatorial Committee of Inquiry declared that the panic imposed ruinous losses upon landed property, which had fallen from a quarter to even a half of its value. In consequence forced sales, bankruptcies, scarcity of money, and a stoppage of work occurred. House-rents fell from $1,200, to $450; the Federal stock alone held its own at 103 to 104.

On the 13th of December, 1819, a Committee of the House of Representatives reported that the panic extended from the greatest to the smallest capitalists. It concluded by demanding the intervention of the legislative power to restrain the corporation, which, spreading its branches throughout the Union had inundated it with nearly $100,000,000, of new circulating medium. Those who unfortunately owed money lost all the fruit of long work, and skilled laborers were obliged to exchange the shelter of their old homes for the inhospitable western forests. Forced sales of provisions, merchandise, and implements were made, greatly below their purchase price. Many families were obliged to limit their most necessary wants. Money and credit were so scarce that it became impossible to obtain a loan upon lands with the securest titles; work ceased with its pay, and the most skilful workman was brought to misery; trade restricted itself to the narrowest wants of life; machinery and manufactories lay idle; the debtor's prison overflowed; the courts of justice were not able to look after their cases, and the wealthiest families could hardly obtain enough money for their daily wants.

The Committee appointed by the Senate of Pennsylvania reported on the 29th of January, 1820, that, to prevent a bad administration of the banks, it was necessary:

1. To forbid them to issue more **than** half of their capital in notes.

2. To divide with the State all dividends in excess of 6 per cent.

3. Excepting the president, that no director should be re-appointed until after an interval of three years.

4. To submit to the State's inspection the bank's business and books.

From this period excessive profits and losses ceased on the part of the American banks. The change of directory of the National Bank, called forth by the unfortunate experience of 1818, was the beginning of a very fortunate epoch. As was always the case, business affairs resumed their usual course when liquidation ceased. Among the various causes assigned for the panic, the increase of import duties had to be pointed out, and the decrease of the Public Debt which was reduced between 1817 and 1818 more than $80,000,000.

It was impossible to turn any portion of the public deposits in proper time either into Federal stock or such other forms of value as its creditors might demand, without shaking or breaking down any respectable institution whatever. But these seem to be only secondary causes.

Panic of 1825 to 1826.—In 1824 in Pennsylvania there was a new rage for banks, and in 1825 there was a repetition of the marvellous days of 1815. American banking bubbles have always been exactly similar to the English South Sea bubble, and to Law's bank in France. In July, after an advance dating from 1819, there was a reaction, a panic, and liquidation. Here we cannot point out any of the causes which we have indicated above; the growth of trade and the exaggeration of discount sufficiently explain the difficulties of the situation.

In Pennsylvania in 1824 a bill was passed re-establishing the charters of all the banks which had failed in 1814. In New York they thought of banks alone; companies with a capital of $52,000,000 were formed. Ready money had never been so abundant, if we can judge of it by the amount of subscriptions and the great speculations in stocks.

Three millions were subscribed to the "New Jersey Protection Company" in one day. But in July, when the decline on the London market was reported, the want of hard money forced itself into notice. Exchange on England rose from 5 per cent. to 10 per cent.; the discount on New Orleans notes, from 3 per cent. became 50 per cent., and on the 4th of December it had fallen back to 4 per cent. What fluctuation ! What disasters !

Mr. Biddle, the President of the United States Stock Bank, said that the crisis of 1825 was the most severe that England had ever experienced, superinduced as it was by the wild American speculation in cottons and mines. Cotton cloth fell from 18 to 13 cents per yard ; and out of 4,000 weavers employed in Philadelphia in 1825 not more than 1,000 remained. The reaction of liquidation was experienced in 1826, and from 1827 money was abundant.

Embarrassment of the Local Banks in 1828 to 1829.—Is it necessary to mention these embarrassments ? The trouble of 1828 affected only the local banks and not at

all those of the United States. The chief
cause was the Bank of the United States'
increase of circulation from August, 1822,
to August, 1828. From $5,400,000 it had
become $13,000,000 without adding any-
thing to the circulation, merely displacing
an equal amount of local bank notes through
drafts of branches that it put into circulation. These branch banks' drafts were in
form of bank notes, signed by the chief
employees of the branches, drawn, it might
be, on each other or on the main bank. A
great issue of paper was thus brought
about; without this roundabout method
it would have been impossible to have
forced the issue of the notes from the mere
physical inability of the president and
cashier to sign so large a number. Congress had always refused to delegate this
power to any other persons; in consequence
of this practice the inevitable result occurred in 1828, as might have been foreseen,
and a conflict between notes of the Bank
of the United States and that of the local
banks occurred.

These drafts circulated everywhere; the

branch banks received them on deposit, but did not redeem them : hence it was necessary to guard against panic by keeping hold of cash. This course increased the issue of the Bank of the United States, and of the local banks which discounted the paper of the central bank as if it were so much cash. The local banks, then, whose paper did not widely circulate, exchanged their bank notes for drafts, thus reducing the amount of circulation of the first, increasing that of the central bank, and hence that of the total issue of its bank notes ; the local banks continued to exchange their paper with its narrow and limited circulation for drafts of this latter, which passed everywhere.

There occurred, then, in 1828 and 1829 an accidental and very brief scarcity of cash, whose cause we have just indicated; but since the second half of the year difficulties arising from metallic circulation had disappeared.

Panic of 1831.—The course of business, having scarcely suffered a stoppage, continued until 1831, and not till then did embarrassment occur (Oct. 8, 1831). Until then business operations were very active and money easy; the revolution in Europe rendered capital available in America, whilst the cholera and the revolution restrained the importation of foreign goods. Discounts at the central bank rose from $24,000,000 in 1826 to $44,000,000 in 1831, and the circulation from $9,000,000 to $22,000,000. The same increase was observable in the banks of the different States.

In March, 1830, the Bank of the United States had in its vaults $8,000,000, which was more than it had ever had before.

In 1829 the Bank of New York claimed to have so much money that it did not know what to do with it. In 1829, 1830, 1831, the banks extended their operations, and a rise in prices accompanied the ease of getting credit; but in November, 1831, very urgent demands for money were heard.

The branch drafts, exchanged with the local banks, allowed them to increase their circulation and consequently their dis-

counts.   American writers boasted greatly
about the assistance the Bank of the
United States yielded both to business and
the nation.   Nevertheless, in 1829, President Jackson declared the conduct of the
Bank to be such that its usefulness had
been justly doubted by many citizens, and
that the end desired, a uniform and regular
circulation, had not been reached.   The
Senate and the House of Representatives
appointed a commission that expressed an
opinion contrary to that of the President.

Panic of 1837 to 1839.—In the midst of
all these troubles the Secretary of the
Treasury informed the President of the
Bank in 1832 that the Government intended, wherever it had representatives, to
redeem half of the 3 per cent. stocks by
paying each holder for half of his certificates.   The President answered that at
that time (March 29th) this redemption from
the European creditors would very greatly
embarrass home business, and that therefore
delay was necessary. He requested a delay of
three months, because trade circles of New
York had already received large advances.

The Bank, being the agent of the Treasury and having $11,600,000 on deposit, would have been forced to become a borrower in order to pay out the $2,700,000 demanded from it. However, its request was granted.

Jackson soon learned with surprise that, business being more impeded than ever, the President had despatched an agent to England to contract with the Barings a loan of $6,000,000. Seeing the Bank to be insolvent he resolved not to renew its charter. The Bank tried to hide its insolvency by the most foolish land speculations, which had already caused such great disaster in 1818 and 1820. The issue of bank notes had given fresh spirit to speculation. These bank notes were received by the National Treasury and returned to the Bank on deposit, which again loaned them to pay for land upon security of the land sold, with the result that the credit granted the Nation was merely fictitious.

In 1832, Congress having voted for the extension of the Bank's charter, President

Jackson refused to ratify it on account especially of certain changes it sought to introduce. "Why," said he, "grant a capital of $35,000,000 when the first company only had $11,000,000 ? "

But though the Bank's charter could not be arranged, the law of July 10, 1832, dealing with the regulation of banks, prescribed that "a report" upon their exact condition should be submitted to Congress every year.

In 1833 General Jackson ordered the withdrawal of the Government deposits from the Bank. The law required that the reasons for the withdrawal of the deposits should be given, and the secretary, Mr. Duane, refused to give them, saying the Bank was not insolvent. He was dismissed and replaced by a more amenable secretary. The deposits were withdrawn and placed in different State Banks. The Bank of the United States was obliged to limit its discounts and loans, thus causing trouble : however, the President wished at any loss to establish a metallic circulation.

Congress was busy through the whole session of 1833–1834 upon the withdrawal of the deposits from the Bank. The Senate sided with the Bank and condemned the President's resolution: the House of Representatives, on the contrary, approved his conduct. The Bank stopped its dealings with the Government in 1836: the President, Mr. Biddle, whom the stockholders had complimented by presenting him a silver service, obtained through a gift of $10,000,000, whose distribution was entirely shrouded in mystery, the especial charter of the Bank of Pennsylvania. He was unwilling to render any account to Congress, notwithstanding reiterated demands. His charter terminated in 1836, and two years after he no longer had the right to transact any business.

When they had obtained the extension of the charter of the Bank of Pennsylvania, the Directors apparently gave no attention to paying their obligations to the Government ($16,000,000). They had turned over books, papers, notes, and engagements to the new corporation, which opened as a successor to the former one.

They had already put bank notes in circulation, despite a notification to redeem them, and to destroy those which remained in their hands.

President Jackson and his successor, Van Buren, considered the excessive issue of paper money as the principal cause of the panic, as well as of the overdoing of every branch of trade, of the boundless speculations, the increase of foreign debts, of imprudent land speculations, and of the alarming increase of a luxury fatal to the springs of industry and to the morality of the people. President Van Buren said that the $30,000,000 entrusted to the Bank had fostered lawless speculations. He strained every effort to re-establish metallic circulation: the banks whose notes were below $5 were no longer recognized by the National Treasury. Until the 3d of March, 1837, it was allowable to make payments with $10 notes, after that time with $20, and finally the banks were only to accept notes whose exchange was at par.

President Adams favored small paper notes of 25 to 10 cents, to the extent of $1,000,000. From 1831 to 1837, $3,400,000 twenty-five cent notes, $5,187,000 ten-cent notes, and $9,771,000 five-cent notes were issued. To prevent an abuse of this it was necessary to resume a metallic circulation immediately. In 1833 the amount of small notes issued had already reached $37,000,000; in 1837 it became $73,000,000; it even exceeded these figures; it was this circulation of small paper notes that had to be made smaller than $120,000,000.

Notwithstanding these frequent panics the national prosperity and the increase of wealth were unquestionable and astonished all observers.

From 1817 to 1834 the national expenses diminished from $39,000,000 to $24,000,000, decreasing even to $14,000,000 in 1835, while the income grew to $37,000,000.

From 1826 to 1836 the condition of business, despite the panic of 1831, grew easier. Industries, agriculture, and commerce were prosperous and every enterprise was successful. Both in New Orleans and in New York there was much building, and more than 1508 houses were erected between January 1 and September 1, 1836. This general prosperity carried with it the seeds of trouble.

The rapid increase of the National revenue gave birth to the belief that capital had increased in the same proportion. This superabundance of income produced temporarily by the inflation in business was recklessly thrown away. People speculated in land, projected a hundred railroads, canals, mines, and every sort of scheme, which would have absorbed $300,-000,000 if carried out.

The national capital being insufficient, loans were made in England and Holland, where the rate of interest being more moderate stimulated the passion for enterprises. Finally, in order to stop the flow of English capital to America, the Bank of England raised the rate of interest; this brought people to their senses. They saw the impossibility of carrying out a third of their schemes. Cotton fell, and panic seized the public.

Since 1818 a period of flow and ebb in trade had been seen every five or six years, but this stoppage was much more serious. The lack of ready money and capital destroyed confidence. Money was not to be had upon any collateral; and the banks stopped discounting. The people lacked bread, the streets were deserted, the theatres empty; social observances were in abeyance, there were no more concerts, and the whole social round was stopped.

The Bank of the United States used various expedients to temporarily moderate the crisis until the very moment that it burst all the more violently in 1839, and brought about a new and radical reform.

From the time that the separation of the Bank of the United States from the Government and the cessation of its operations as the National Bank was brought about, the quotation on bank notes considerably decreased, as well for those payable at sight as for the deferred notes payable in twelve months. The President sent an agent to London to raise money upon the bank shares.

Fearing that General Jackson would not establish a new bank, and by way of counterpoise, one hundred banks were created with a capital of more than $125,000,000; issues of bank stock were not to exceed three times the amount of the capital, but this provision was not observed; the issue was without regulation and without limits, and during an inflation in prices of the necessaries of life which had doubled in value, and which had turned the people's attention to agriculture. The price of land had for some time advanced tenfold, and the advance in cotton caused the Southern planters to abandon indigo and rice.

Imports in 1836 exceeded the exports by $50,000,000, which had to be paid in gold or silver. This outflow of metal created a great void.

The advance in the discount rate in the Bank of England under such circumstances came like a thunder-clap, and the distended bladder burst. Banks suspended payment, and bank notes lost from 10 to 20 per cent. Exchange on France and England rose to 22 per cent., all metal disappeared from circulation, and a thousand failures took place. The English export houses lost from £5,000,000 to £6,000,000 sterling; values fell from maximum to minimum. The losses in America were even greater; cotton fell to nothing. At the worst of the panic people turned to the Bank of the United States, and its President, being examined as to the means of remedying the trouble, stated that it was above all necessary to maintain the credit of the Bank of England in stead and in place of private credit, which had disappeared. He proposed to pay everything in bank paper on Paris, London, and Amsterdam.

When the panic came the Bank was very much shaken. At the beginning of April, 1837, the New York banks suspended payments because demands for hard money for export played the chief rôle; the other banks suspended in their turn, promising to resume with them.

The Bank of the United States suspended also, Mr. Biddle, the President, asserting that it would have continued to pay were it not for the injury done by New

York. This was false, for the New York banks shortly after resumed payment, hoping they would be imitated, but the other banks refused to do so. Mr. Biddle wished, in the first place, to await the result of the harvest. To uphold the Bank, he tried to bring about exchanges, both with banks and general business, not only in America but in Europe, in order to establish a unity of interests which would sustain him and conceal his real condition. In this he was successful to a certain degree, for in 1840 in his balance sheet $53,000,000 of paper of the different States was shown up. He wished above all to secure the monopoly of the sale of cotton: a senseless speculation hitherto unexampled,[1] the like of which may never be seen again.

Whilst the Bank came to the relief of New York business through its exchange and its deferred notes, Biddle posed as the great cotton agent, on condition that the Bank's agents should be consigned to at Havre and Liverpool. In their embar-

[1] A similar episode has occurred in our time in the speculation in metals by the "Comptoir d'Escompte."

rassment this proposition was accepted by the planters. Cotton was thus accumulated in those two places. This monopoly advanced the price, and vast sums were realized, which enabled him to enlarge the scope of his business. In 1837 he was enabled by this means to draw on London for £3,000,000 sterling; the difference between 5 to 6 per cent. interest and discount at 2 per cent. produced a very handsome profit. The cotton merchants prospered as well as the exchange agent, and Mr. Biddle paid the planters in bank notes which the Bank could furnish without limit, while he received in Europe hard money for the cotton; this aroused opposition.

In the second half of 1837 he established in Missouri, Arkansas, Alabama, Georgia, and Louisiana a number of new banks, to make advances to the planters, and to sell their products for them in Europe. They started with very slight capital, they observed no rules in issuing paper, their bank notes fell 30 per cent. in 1838, and the planters would not take them.

The Bank of the United States, fearing lest foreign capitalists should take advantage of the difficulties of the planters by buying this cotton, cheapened on account of the encumbrances upon the district producing it, resolved to come to the rescue of the Southern banks, and to join them in their operations by purchasing their shares and their long-time paper, having two years to run. It thus put $100,000,000 into the business, and in 1838 it had loaned them upon their cotton crops not less than $20,000,000 at 7 per cent., payable in three years.

It had bought the bank shares at 28 per cent. below par; through its help they had risen again to par; and then it threw them upon the London market, which absorbed them. In order to explain the immense credit enjoyed in Europe by the United States and their banks, we must observe that the extinguishment of the National obligations through surplus crops threw a false light upon the credit of the States, as well as particularly upon that of the corporation. For many years American investments had been sought for above all others in London, and as nothing happened during the first year to destroy that confidence, the amount thus employed increased from \$150,000,000 to \$200,000,-000 in 1840. In Pennsylvania \$16,000,000 of European money was used in the Bank of the United States, and \$40,000,000 in those of the different States, all of which was payable in two or three years.

Mr. Biddle had succeeded in sustaining the different States with the National credit. He knew how to utilize the credit of American goods in Europe, and drew from the London market an immense sum against exchange long-time paper and paper payable in America. The Bank's paper fell from 4 to 6 per cent., and it was in such demand that the Bank of England took it at 2 to 3 per cent. discount. But finally the market had all that it could take. The attention of merchants was attracted to Mr. Biddle's gigantic speculations, who paid paper in America and collected hard money in London: Business interests complained about the contraction in the market. The Bank's stock of cotton increased steadily, and between June and July it rose from fifty-eight to ninety million bales.

This speculation had already yielded $15,000,000 profit, but the market was overloaded, and quotations could not keep up. The planters had made a great deal by the advance in cotton, but the paper money remitted them lost from 15 to 25 per cent. A panic was approaching. The cotton crop, amounting to 400,000 bales, was one fifth less than was expected ; they awaited an advance in price, but the contrary occurred. The high prices had brought out all the stored cotton ; the factories had reduced their work. Nevertheless bale after bale was forwarded to Liverpool and to Havre. The sale in this last port in February and March, 1839, having produced a loss, they continued to store it. As soon as Mr. Biddle was aware of this stoppage he sought to hide the difficulty by extending his business. He proposed to start a new bank in New York (the other had headquarters in Philadel-

phia) with a capital of $50,000,000. He
once more issued long-time paper, and
bought with American paper canals, railroads, and shares which he threw upon the
English market. This lasted until the
long-time paper lost 18 per cent. in
America, and until American exchange and
investments were no longer received on the
Continent.

The Parisian house of Hottinguer like
its other agents, sold little until the first of
July, and when it saw that the effort to
monopolize cotton could not succeed, fearing to continue this gigantic operation, it
declared that it employed too much capital.
In the midst of all this, some new bills of
exchange reached Paris without consign-
ment of corresponding value; and the house
of Hottinguer protested.

Hope of Amsterdam discontinued his
connection. The London agent called upon
the Bank of England for help, which was
granted upon the guaranty of certain firms
of that place and a deposit of good American paper.

Rothschild accepted the refused bills of

exchange, after having found out that a sum of £400,000 would suffice for Mr. Biddle's agent; these £400,000 offered as a guaranty consisted of Government stock, and of shares in railroads, canals, and banks. This agreement was not given out freely, which still further increased the feeling of distrust. A crisis in which $150,000,000 of European capital were destined to be engulfed was rapidly approaching.

Breaking out of the Panic of 1839.—The English papers had already warned the people to be distrustful. The *Times* said it was impossible to have any confidence in the Bank as long as it would not resume specie payments. Mr. Biddle defended himself through papers paid for the purpose, finally in the Augsburg *Gazette*, while he waited for the soap bubble to burst. His retained defenders claimed that the 150,000 bales of cotton sent to Europe had not been sold, but received on commission. Advances in paper had been made which in the month of August, 1839, were to be paid in notes by the Southern banks, for a new grant made to the Bank

by the State of Pennsylvania permitted it
to buy the shares of other banks, and by
this means to gain their management;
their notes lost 20 to 50 per cent. as compared with the Northern banks.

Through his profit upon the difference of
the notes, and through the payment for the
cotton in paper, and through the sale of
bullion exchange, Mr. Biddle had made five
to six million dollars, which lay at his com-
mand in London.

The protection of his bills of exchange
made a great impression in England; the
rebound was felt in America, where the
panic, moderated in 1837 through the intervention of the Bank, burst forth with
renewed fury in 1839, and brought about
the complete liquidation of that establish-
ment.

At the same time the English market
was very much pressed, for, according to a
notice of the Chamber of Commerce, the
number of that year's bankruptcies was
greater than usual. From June 11, 1838
to June, 1839, there were 306 bankruptcies
in London, and 781 in the "provinces,"—in

all, 1,087. At Manchester there were 82, at
Birmingham 54, at Liverpool 44, at Leeds
33. The London Exchange was flooded
with unsalable paper, an occurrence which
had also taken place on a smaller scale in
1837.

Such was the interruption of business
that interest for money rose to 20 per cent.,
and the discount rate for the best paper to
15 or 18 per cent.

The various States in the Union had
contracted debts with inconceivable ease,
and interest payments were provided for
by new loans. President Jackson declared it necessary to make a loan in order
to pay interest moneys. It was deemed
inexpedient to impose new taxes to provide for the cost of the public works.
Great was the embarrassment in America,
and as no more money came from England,
it was necessary for the Americans to look
for it in their own country.

Business circles were flooded with long-
time paper running at a discount of one
half of 1 per cent. a month. Discount
rose to 25 per cent. The panic was so

great that all confidence was destroyed.
The Bank of the United States, in order
to maintain its credit, paid its depreciated
long-time paper.

The struggle between the Bank and its
opponents, led by President Van Buren,
re-commenced. These last declared that
the Bank had erred in circulating the
$4,000,000 of notes of the old bank, which
should have been retired coincidently with
the charter; and the Senate forbade their
circulation.

The Government claimed large sums
from the Bank, the statement of which
showed close to $4,000,000; and, as it
could not secure this amount in money, it
was decided to issue $10,000,000 of Treas-
ury bonds. The Bank party wished to
push the Government into bankruptcy, in
order to induce it to turn to them for help,
and, through the issue of " circular specie,"
oblige it to adopt a system of paper money.

A bill was brought forward with this
view. Biddle, who wished to increase the
circulation, said he could resume specie
payments, and thus forced his shares to

rise; but the rejoicing of the Bank party was soon disturbed by the fact that collectors of taxes were forbidden to receive any bank note for less than $20, which was not redeemable in hard money.

After a struggle of eight years the separation became complete, and the administration of National finances was withdrawn from the Bank.

In 1836, a law was passed providing that upon the expiration of its charter, the National funds should be again deposited with it, as soon as the Bank resumed specie payment. Upon the suspension in 1837, the Government was forced to abate the law, in order to protect the specie, and imposed on its financial and postal agents some of the duties of the Treasury. In 1840, the management of the public Treasury constituted a separate and distinct department. Such was the liquidation following the panic, that Congress granted the Bank three months in which it must either resume specie payment or liquidate. To conform to this decree the State of Pennsylvania fixed the resumption of

specie payments by its banks, for January
15, 1841. The shares of the Bank, which
had yielded no dividend in 1839, and
offered a similar outlook for the first half
of 1840, fell to $61. They had been
quoted as high as $1,500. General liqui-
dation and a loss of 50 per cent. was inevitable. This occurred in 1841. Thus
ceased for a time the bank mania in the
United States.

We will recall here Buchanan's opinion
about the Bank: "If the Bank of the
United States, after ceasing to be a
national bank, and obtaining a new
charter in Pennsylvania, had restrained
itself to legitimate banking, had used its
resources to regulate the rate of home exchange, and had done everything to hasten
the resumption of specie payments, it
would have resurrected the National Bank.

"But this is no longer possible; it has
defied Congress, violated the laws, and is
mixed up in politics. The people have
recognized the viciousness of its administration; the President, Mr. Biddle, has
concluded the work Jackson began."

Tables indicating the banks which suspended during the panic : In 1814, 90 ; in 1830, 165 ; in 1837, 618 ; in 1839, 959.

The last panic, from 1837 to 1839, produced, according to some pretty accurate reports of 1841, 33,000 failures, involving a loss of $440,000,000.

Panic of 1848.—The entire discounts, which had risen to $525,000,000 in 1837, fell to $485,000,000 in 1838, only to rise again to $492,000,000 in 1839, and the real liquidation of the panic occurred only then. Discounts fell at once to $462,000,-000, then $386,000,000 ; the abundance of capital, and the low price at which it was offered, cleared out bank paper until it was reduced from $525,000,000 to $254,-000,000 in 1843.[1]

The metallic reserve increased from $37,000,000 to $49,000,000 (1844); the circulation was reduced from $149,000,000 to $58,000,000.

The number of banks in 1840, from 901 fell to 691 in 1843, and the capital itself

---

[1] We have not the outside figures, the maximum or minimum.

from $350,000,000 in 1840 was reduced to $200,000,000 in 1845 and to even $196,-000,000 in 1846.

All these figures clearly indicate liquidation. The market, freed from its exchange, was enabled to permit affairs to resume their ordinary course.

In fact an upward movement was taking place. Discounts rose from $264,000,000 to $344,000,000 in 1848.

Banks increased from 691 in 1843 to 751 in 1848, and their capital grew from $196,000,000 in 1846 to $207,000,000. The paper circulation rose from $58,000,-000 to $128,000,000 in 1848. Deposits from $62,000,000 reached $103,000,000 in 1848. The metallic reserve alone fell from $49,000,000 in 1844 to $35,000,000 in 1848.

The consequences of the European panic were felt in America, but without causing much trouble. The liquidation of the panic of 1839 was barely over, and was still too recent to have permitted sufficient extension of business

Embarrassments were slight and brief;

.discounts, nevertheless, fell from $344,000,-000 to $332,000,000.

The store of bullion, in spite of the surplus and the favorable balance produced by the export of grain to Europe, fell from $49,000,000 to $35,000,000; with the following year the forward movement recommenced.

Panic in 1857.—The stoppage in 1848 was very brief. Discounts rose regularly from $332,000,000 to $364,000,000, $413,-000,000, $557,000,000, $576,000,000, $634,-000,000, and finally $684,000,000 in 1857. The progression was irresistible. The circulation rose from $114,000,000 to $214,-000,000. The banks increased at such a rate that, from 707 in 1846, with a capital of $196,000,000, there were in 1857 1416, whose capital had risen to $370,000,000,—a very inferior figure, in comparison to the number of banks, to that of 1840, when 901 banks only had a capital of $358,-000,000.

The metallic reserve, from $35,000,000 in 1847, easily reached $59,000,000 in 1856: but it was in proportion neither

with the number of the banks nor their
discounts and circulation ; and, after all,
this is only a moderate sum. We have
not the extreme maximum or minimum,
and the suspension of specie payments
took place notwithstanding the amount of
cash on hand, which was greater in 1857
than in 1856.

Deposits accumulated from $91,000,000
to $230,000,000 ; they rose to their greatest
height in the very year of the crisis ; nevertheless, they could not be drawn out.

During the Eastern war the prosperity
of the United States had been so great
that the clearing-houses established in New
York in 1853, and in Boston in 1855,
offered only a slight opposition to the
excessive issue : at least, in 1837 the Congressional report stated the cash on hand
was $6,500,000—that is to say, $1.00 in
metal to each $6.00 in paper.

In 1857 cash on hand was $14,300,000, or
$1.00 in hard money for each $8.00 in paper.

The banks had attracted deposits by
high interest, and loaned the money to
wild speculators. On the 22d of August,

1857, the amount of loans had become al-most $12,000,000, counting together metal, notes, and deposits.

From December, 1856, to June, 1857, they had shown great strength. Discounts had risen from $183,000,000 to $190,000,-000 in June; cash on hand had risen from $11,000,000 to $14,000,000. The only evi-dence of weakness, so to speak, was that the withdrawal of deposits had risen from $94,000,000 to $104,000,000, while the cir-culation diminished $1,000,000.

In June "the position of the Bank ought not to have caused any fear, to the most far-sighted," says the report of the Com-mittee of Inquiry.

Foreign exchange was favorable, and it is known that is the bankers' guide. June, July, and August were tranquil, except for a slight disturbance in business experi-enced by the country bankers through the constantly increasing amount of notes pre-sented for redemption, and among the city bankers by requests for discount.

The collapse of the " Ohio Life," which had the best New York connection, was the first muttering of the storm, and was soon followed by the suspension of the Mechanics' Banking Association, one of the oldest banks in the country. The suspension of the Pennsylvania and Maryland banks followed. Public confidence remained unshaken — it relied upon the circulating medium.

Only one bank went to protest, and that on September 4th, on a $250 demand. Another protest followed on the 12th, a third on the 15th, both for insignificant amounts. Demands in the way of withdrawal amounted to almost nothing, and there was nothing like a panic.

The deposits at the savings banks were a little less, but this did not continue. Only at the close of September was the demand by the country banks for payment upon the Metropolitan American Exchange Bank for payment greater than it had ever been.

On the 13th of October, with exchange at par, an abundant harvest, with a premium of $\frac{1}{4}$ to $\frac{1}{2}$ per cent. on metal, the banks suspended specie payment, but resumed it on the 11th of December. The most critical period lasted about a month. The first step towards resumption of payments was made after the resolution adopted by the Committee of Liquidation to call upon the country banks to redeem the notes of the Metropolitan Bank, paying an allowance of $\frac{1}{4}$ of 1 per cent. interest, running from the 20th of November.

At this time the city bankers held, in bills issued and in signed parcels of $5,000 each, about $7,000,000 due by the country banks. They were thus enabled to accomplish the payment of their notes at the rate of 20 per cent. a month by the 1st of January, 1858. The same favor of repaying their notes at the rate of 6 per cent. was granted to the city banks.

We need not inquire if, having granted this delay, the banks proved their liberality. The abundant harvest also assisted liquidation.

From 1853 to 1857 the metallic reserve fell to $7,000,000, deposits rose to $99,000,000, and discounts and loans to $122,000,000.

BANKS OF NEW YORK.

	Metallic Reserve.	Deposits.	Discounts, Advances.	Proportion of the Metallic Reserve to Deposits.
1854....	$15,000,000	$ 58,000,000	$ 80,000,000	26 %
1855....	9,900,000	85,000,000	101,000,000	11 %
1856....	10,000,000	100,000,000	112,000,000	10 %
1857....	7,000,000	99,000,000	122,000,000	7 %

The reduction of the metallic reserve, increase of deposits and of discounts and of advances, are here clearly indicated.

From 1853 to 1857 the bank circulation hardly varied $100,000, indicating that the demand for hard money came from abroad and from the interior. The circulation was not the cause of the suspension,—at least such was the opinion expressed by the superintendent of the New York banks in his report.

In 1856 twenty-five companies were started, and three bankers opened business with a capital of $7,500,000, of which $7,200,000, was paid in.

In 1857 there were only five of these banks and three bankers having a capital of $6,000,000, of which only $4,000,000 were paid in. The collateral deposited by the banks represented $2,500,000 in 1856, on which credit of $2,000,000 in notes was granted.

In 1857 the same collateral did not exceed $560,000 estimated value, on which a credit of $383,000 in paper was granted.

At the height of the crisis failures were so numerous that a general suspension of payments, and, in consequence, a stoppage of business was dreaded. This suspension, in place of being general, turned out to be merely partial; it occurred at a juncture when it might well be feared that it would lead on to the very greatest disasters, but, far from harming, it helped the market. The banks had suspended payment upon a common understanding among themselves and with business circles. The critical moment having passed, tranquillity reappeared as soon as the course determined on was known.

If suspension of payment hurts the credit of a bank, it does not necessarily lead to the depreciation of its bank notes.

There are a good many proofs of this: in 1796, when the Bank of England suspended, its bank notes did not depreciate; and if this state of things did not last, the blame must be laid upon the excessive issue. And in France, in 1848 as well as in 1871, the Bank of France suspended without the depreciation of its bank notes becoming very noticeable. So, in New York, bank notes passed at 2 or 3 per cent. loss at this crisis.

The crisis disappeared with the end of the year, and resumption of payments took place between New York and Hamburg, with the return of specie and a rate of 4 per cent.

It was the same in France and England. A more serious panic and a more rapid recovery had never been seen. The rigidness and not the severity of the pressure that had to be exercised shows the condition of business. There had been most blamable practices employed; but the market as a whole was sound, and had faced the storm.

Only four banks had suspended, three of which were shaky before the panic, and the fourth had already resumed payments.

At no other period could one have obtained such an amount of credit upon a simple paper circulation; fictitious paper was the source of all the wrecks. To get it into circulation the most varied contrivances were resorted to, and fraud itself was not wanting; the signatures even became fictitious, their owners could not be found. Shams and discriminations under all forms, designed to permit speculation without capital, without exchange of goods, without real transactions between the drawer and the acceptor of the bill of exchange, were rife.

In his message, President Buchanan ascribed the crisis to the vicious system of the fiduciary circulation, and to the extravagant credits granted by the banks, although he was aware that Congress had no power to curb these excesses. When there is too much paper, when the public has created an endless chain of bank notes, representing no real value, it is enough that the first ring break for the whole gear, thus no longer held together, to fall to pieces.

If we mark the situation of the New York banks before and during the panic—

that is to say, in 1852 and in 1857, we will ascertain as follows:

	June, 1852.	June, 1856.	June, 1857.
Capital	$ 59,700,000	$ 92,300,000	$107,500,000
Circulation......	27,900,000	30,700,000	27,100,000
Deposits	65,600,000	96,200,000	84,500,000
Paper discounted	127,000,000	174,100,000	170,800,000
Cash on hand...	13,300,000	18,500,000	14,300,000

This table demonstrates that two items show a great increase: capital increased $47,000,000 and paper discounted $43,000,000; while, in face of an increase of $1,000,000 of specie on hand, the note circulation decreased $800,000.

Far from finding a mistake, we find a proof of the Directors' prudence. If there was an error in the issuing of paper, it was not on the side of the banks; it was the public itself that was chiefly in fault.

We find the causes of the panic in the issues of railway obligations and shares, which had chiefly been placed in European markets, and whose gross amount was estimated at £1,000,000. The speculation in land and railroads had been carried on either with borrowed money or by open credits, and by accommodation notes, back of which there was no second party.

The mistake of the banks was in trying to conduct their whole business by their note circulation and to concentrate their capital in the bank offices, and meanwhile, as they refused to loan to the stockholders of the banks, discounts in New York fell off $10,000,000. Finally the capital could not be entrusted to the disposal of the banks and it was necessary to compel them to make a deposit of $100,000 for each association, and $50,000 for each banker.

Such were the final advices given by the inspector-general of the banks of New York at the close of his report, dealing with how to prevent the recurrence of panics. To have confidence in their efficacy, it was necessary to forget the past and its lessons.

The reforms already made and those still asked for in the bank system could yield no remedy for those abuses lying beyond legislative action. The American news-papers did not hesitate to demand them, well aware that they would produce no effect; however, they congratulated them-selves with having drawn away from effete

Europe one million sterling now realized upon the soil of the United States without any equivalent given for it to the foreign lenders.

Panic of 1864.—The crisis of 1864 was mixed up in the United States with the War of Secession ; it was a political crisis, and is not properly to be considered here.

Panic of 1873.—During the last two months of 1872 the American market had been very much embarrassed ; the lowest rate of discount was 7 per cent., and in December it was quoted at even $\frac{1}{32}$ of 1 per cent. or a quarter of 1 per cent. a day !

The year 1873 was anxiously awaited in hope of better times. In the middle of January, 1873, the rate of interest declined a little to 6 or 7 per cent., but soon the rate of $\frac{1}{32}$ of 1 per cent. per day reappeared and continued until the month of May.

In the first days of April the market was in full panic ; it grew steadier in the first week of May, and in the month following. It relapsed on September 1st, and requests for accommodation redoubled until the

sharpest moment of the panic. On that day
there were no quoted rates; money could
not be had at any price: some few loans
were made at 1½ per cent. per day.

This panic broke forth on September
18th, through the failure of Jay Cooke,
after a miserable year, during which money
was constantly sought for and was held at
very high prices in all branches of business.
As to the loans for building railroads, they
followed one another so rapidly that, from
the month of October, 1871, to the month
of May, 1873, they could not be placed at
a lower rate than 7 per cent. Bankers
succumbed beneath the burden of their unsalable issues. This was a grave misfor-
tune for the railroads. In the single year
1873 there were constructed 4,190 miles of
railroad in the United States, which, at
$29,000 per mile, represented the enormous
sum of $121,000,000, and in the last five
years $1,700,000,000.

The commercial situation was not so
bad, and the number of failures did not
reach the proportion that might have been
feared.

After the failure of Jay Cooke came those of Fiske & Hatch, of the Union Trust Company, of the National Trust Company, and of the National Bank of the Commonwealth. On the 20th of September, for the first time, the Stock Exchange in New York City was closed for ten days, during which legal-tender notes were at a premium of ¼ per cent. to 3 per cent. above certified cheques.

On the 18th there was a run on the deposits. Withdrawals continued on the 19th and 20th, especially by the country banks, and the banks' correspondents. No security could be realized upon; and in order to relieve the situation the Secretary of the Treasury bought $13,500,000 of National 5-20 bonds, stating that he could do no more.

The New York Stock Exchange was reopened September 30th, without any notable occurrence; but everything was very low. Several other suspensions occurred— for instance, that of Sprague, Claflin, & Co.

The rate of discount being 9 per cent., a panic was feared in London. The banks passed the most critical period on October 14th; out of $32,278,000 legal-tender dollars at the beginning of the panic, only $5,800,000 remained on hand. Not until the middle of November did the decline stop and a slight advance take place.

Throughout the panic the bank reserves were much below the legal requirement of 25 per cent.; from the 13th to the 20th of September they fell to 24.44 and 23.55 per cent.

The New York Clearing House in September adopted a measure which permitted dealings to continue. It authorized the banks to deposit the bills on hand, or the other securities they had accepted, in exchange for which they issued certificates of deposit bearing 7 per cent. in notes of $5,000 to $10,000 to the extent of 70 per cent. of the security deposited. Thus $26,-565,000 of them were put into circulation.

Furthermore, they made a common fund of the legal tenders belonging to the Associated Banks for mutual aid and protection.

The suspension of payment took place first in New York and then extended to the large cities of the Union; it lasted forty days, until the 1st of November; this measure was looked upon as having pre-vented the greatest disasters.

The table setting forth the situation, compared with the balance sheets of the Associated Banks of New York on January 1st, April 1st, July 1st, September 1st, and October 1st of the years 1870, 1871, 1872, and 1873, shows us the following changes: discounts had fluctuated from $250,000,000 in January, 1870, to $309,000,000 in September, 1871; they had become reduced to $278,000,000 in September, 1873, on the eve of the panic, and from the month of September, liquidation of the panic having begun, they were reduced to $250,000,000. Deposits from $179,000,000 in January, 1870, rose to $248,000,000 in July, 1871, with $296,000,000 of bills discounted, and once more reached $198,000,000 in September, 1873, with $278,000,000 of discounts and $195,000,000 in December.

Even at the most critical moment of the panic they continued larger than the usual average of the preceding years.

The metallic reserves played too feeble a role to have caused failure; they had varied from $34,000,000 in June, 1870, to $9,000,-000 in September, 1871, $18,000,000 in September, 1873, and $23,000,000 in December, 1873.

The circulation varied still less : from $34,000,000 in January, 1876, it decreased to $27,000,000 in July, 1872, and remained at the same figure during the year 1873, if we can judge of this by the balance sheet rendered on the first day of each quarter. In each case there is no opportunity for us to charge an excessive issue.

According to the statement of the Comptroller of the Currency, paper discounted decreased between the 12th of September and the 1st of November from $199,000,000 to $169,000,000.

To sum up, the circulation had fluctuated very little; deposits from $99,000,000 had increased to $167,000,000 between the 12th and 20th of September, at the most critical period ; and when suspension was universal, they had declined to $89,000,000. After the breaking out on the 18th of October, and since then from the 22d of November, they had risen to $138,000,000.

The metallic reserve, after a brief revival from $14,000,000 to $18,000,000 between the 12th and 20th of September, had fallen back to $10,000,000, only to rise to $14,-000,000 in November.

In the midst of these difficulties, the securities of the various States held up. Since the first months of 1873, the demands of the English market caused an upward movement in them; in September it was impossible to make a loan, without using them as collateral. In order to help the market somewhat, the Treasury bought about $13,000,000 of National securities on the Stock Exchange, but, lacking resources, that was the only effort it could make. The German Government invested quite a large sum in the new five per cents, so that the advance in public securities lasted through the whole year: the market rate for 5–20's advanced from 91 per cent. in April to 96 per cent. in October, in the midst of the market's panic.

The $15,000,000 of indemnity awarded by

the Geneva Court of Arbitration, and paid by England for having admitted privateers into her ports, was put into 5–20's. Apart from this strength in the public securities, the railway obligations, especially those upon new roads, were very much depressed; they could no longer be placed, ninety new companies having stopped paying their coupons, whilst those of the old lines held their quotations.

Great speculators, Vanderbilt at the head, formed syndicates, embracing several companies, and made prices as suited their plans. The death of Mr. Clarke in June dealt the first blow to this combination, and the failure of George Bird Grinnell brought about its dissolution.

The liquidation of this tremendous concern kept down prices for a long time.

The price of gold, still quoted at 112½ per cent. in January, 1873, rose to 119½ per cent. in April, superinduced by speculation, for at the height of the panic it declined to 106 on the 6th of November. It is true that at that time all doubtful accounts were liquidated, and demands for gold had disappeared; if we were to rely upon the export figures only, we would find them less than in the preceding years.

Exchange rates were much more depressed; from 109.45, representing par, they fell to 107.25 for the best 60-day paper. This paper was much sought after by speculators, who, when discounting it, procured bonds authorizing them to transfer the titles unless payment was made promptly at maturity. Prices fell so low that it was often impossible to negotiate paper at any price. The activity reigning at the beginning of the year showed itself in the Exchange movement; the excess of imports over exports rose in the first months to $100,000,000, whilst in the preceding year it did not exceed $62,000,000; prices ruling in the American market attracted goods from all quarters.

Panic of 1884.—The panic which burst upon the United States in 1884 was the last thunder-clap of the commercial tempest which had reigned since the month of January, 1882. Public opinion already recalled the decennial period which sepa-

rated the existing panic from that of 1873.
The acute period was of short duration;
the crash occurred on May 14th, and the
decline of values had touched bottom by
the end of June.   From the 9th of June
the people began to steady up, they felt
the ground firmer under their feet.   The
situation gave evidence of great strength;
and, notwithstanding the dearness of money,
and an enormous fall in prices, there were
only a few failures, and at the close of the
year equilibrium was re-established, although the liability of the losses had risen
to $240,000,000.   These losses, it is true,
were almost entirely borne by financiers and
speculators, rather than by manufacturers
and traders.

The month of May, 1884, concludes the
prosperous period which followed the crisis of 1873.   During this period the most
gigantic speculations in railroads occurred;
the zenith of the movement was in 1880,
and as early as 1881 a retrograde movement began, only to end in the disasters in
question.   The decline in prices had been
steady for three years; they had sunk

little by little under the influence of a ruinous competition, caused by the number of new lines and the lowering of rates, but above all through the manipulations by the managers on a scale unexampled until now. In connection with the disasters of May, 1884, the names of certain speculators who misused other people's money, such as Ward, of Grant & Ward; Fish, President of the Marine Bank; and John C. Eno, of the Second National Bank, will long be remembered. General Grant, who was a silent partner in Ward's concern, was an innocent sufferer, both in fortune and reputation.

The Marine Bank suspended on the 5th of May, and in the following week the Metropolitan drew down in its train a large number of bankers and houses of the second order. The confusion was then at its height. Owing to the very delicate mechanism of the credit circulation, the banks and the clearing house were the first attacked and the most shaken, but they immediately formed themselves into a syndicate to resist the storm which was upsetting all about them. As cheques were no longer paid, settlements no longer took place, and the credit circulation was suspended; this stoppage was liable to induce the greatest consequences, hence it was necessary to be very circumspect. Here it was not possible to suspend the law, as in England the Act of 1844 was suspended, permitting an excess of the official limit for the note issue, but the banks could have been empowered to demand authority to change the proportion enacted by the law creating National Banks. They had no recourse to any of these violations of the Statutes, which prove only too often under such circumstances that regulation by law is impossible; they satisfied themselves, without having the public powers intervene, with issuing clearing-house certificates, that is to say, promises, which they were bound to accept as cheques in settling up the operations of each day. It was through this help that the Metropolitan Bank was enabled to resume payments on the 15th of May, the evening of the day following its suspension. The Second National Bank was a loser through the acts of its President, Mr. John C. Eno, but his father and the Directors hastened to make good the deficit. At this moment the excitement was intense, deposits were withdrawn, and 1 per cent. a day was paid, and even more, to obtain ready money or credit; under the influence of numerous sales of securities, exchange fell rapidly, metallic money was secured in London even, to be hurried to New York. Never could purchases be made under better auspices. Above all is this true when we observe that the condition of companies was much better known than in 1873.

The year 1883 had been disturbed by numerous failures. There had been no crash, but prices, far from advancing, had held their own with difficulty. On the eve of the breaking out of the panic there was complaint about the accumulation of goods in the warehouses, and of the difficulty of making exports. No scheme worked out, despite a very high protective tariff, and people were asking themselves what was its effect under the influence of unfavorable exchanges. Gold flowed away from the country, and cash on hand decreased each day.

On the 1st of January, 1884, the New York & New England Railroad was placed in the hands of a receiver by order of the court. The same thing happened on the 12th of January to the North River Company. In February, March, and April many houses exhibited their balance sheets. The fall in prices grew accentuated not only on the Stock Exchange, but in all markets. The discomfort increased until the 6th of May, the day on which occurred the failure of the National Marine Bank, whose President was associated with the house of Grant and Ward, which went down shortly afterwards with a liability of $17,000,000. This financial disaster made a great stir. Anxiety spread everywhere, when on the 13th of May the President of the Second National Bank of New York was also forced to suspend payment with a liability of $3,000,000; this was the final blow to credit. Every operation was suspended, all exchange became impossible; not securities but money was lacking. At one time the panic was such that the rate of discount and loans rose to 4 per cent. a day !

Although the panic was general, it was rather a panic of securities in the chief places of the United States, especially in New York.

One no longer knew on whom to count to provide ready money. Offerings were made on the Stock Exchange where there were no bidders, and the market disappeared in the midst of a panic which paralyzed every one.

This melancholy state of things was still further aggravated on the 14th of May by the failure of Donnel, Lawson, & Simpson and Hatch & Foote. On May 15th it was the turn of the Savings Banks of New York, of Fiske & Hatch, and of many others. It was impossible to obtain any credit from the banks, and all securities were unsalable, unless at ruinous rates. Reduced to such an extremity, it was necessary to adopt some course to help the market and avoid suspension of payments.

The certified checks issued by the banks did not answer, and it was necessary to have recourse to a new means of settlement. The members of the clearing house emerged from their usual passive role to intervene and to do a novel thing: they issued certificates that they accepted in the name of the most embarrassed institutions whose fall they wished to avert, in order to prevent the failure of others. Then, as everybody was making default, the Secretary of the Treasury in his turn wished to aid the common effort to sustain the credit of the situation, and, in order to accomplish this by the most regular methods, he pledged himself to prepay the debt, whose term was close at hand.

Despite these last helps it was easily seen how great must be the disorder, to induce recourse to such methods. Never had they been employed until now, which is proof enough of the enormity of the situation, whose equilibrium had been disturbed since 1887, the year in which high prices in everything had been reached on the Stock Exchange.

To still further increase the joint responsibility of the members of the clearing

house, it was agreed that a committee
should be charged with receiving as collateral bills and securities in exchange for
which certificates of deposit bearing 3 per
cent. were issued at the rate of 75 per cent.
of the amounts deposited. This agreement being adopted, a way to re-open the
National Metropolitan Bank was sought.
A selection made from its collection of
bills showed the securities it could pledge
for clearing-house certificates; and, its circulation being thus re-established, it was
enabled on May 15th to take part in settlements.

Upon the announcement of a syndicate
composed of the banks and the clearing
house, things settled down; the general
distrust diminished; there was the necessity
and wish to realize, but funds were lacking.

The rise in the discount rate attracted
foreign capital little by little, and exchange
grew easier. With the help of the syndicate the credit circulation became re-established, and the rate of discount declined to
5 per cent. For commercial needs money

was always to be had at 4½ per cent. and
at 5 per cent. when at the Stock Exchange
it was necessary to pay 4 per cent. per
day!

The panic was terrible from the 3d to
the 10th of May; for two days no one
wished to part with his money; it was impossible to borrow on any collateral, at
any price whatever. Hence came a decline
in the public securities, which fell below
the low prices of 1873.

The public complained that it could not
have foreseen the panic, because the loss of
gold had been concealed by the oft-repeated
assurance that there was a reserve of $600,-
000,000 in Washington.

Similar situations in 1857 and in 1873
were recalled, and it was remarked that
like troubles had not occurred until after a
long period of high prices, when capital
was scarce and the rate of interest high,
whereas this was far from being the case
at this period.

It was nevertheless notorious that the
decline in prices began two years back, that
the advance in prices had been stopped by

the breaking out of the panic of 1882 in
Europe, at Paris, and that since that
moment prices had begun to decline, less
rapidly, however, than in Europe, because
the shock had then merely disturbed a
market which had not yet recovered from
the panic of 1873, from which, in consequence of the Franco-Prussian war, France
had escaped. The mine not being sufficiently charged in the United States the
explosion had not recurred. Speculation,
unable to restore a new impulse to the rise
in prices, was nevertheless able to hold its
own, until May, 1884, when the delayed
explosion finally occurred, covering the
market with ruins and bringing about a
liquidation with its accustomed train, a
great and lengthy decline of prices.

We may here note similar delays in the
breaking out of panics, in the period of
1837, 1839, 1864–1866 in France and in
England. Even an involved state of affairs
may be hidden by certain conditions, and
the situation, although itself exposed to the
same excessive speculation, may witness
the breaking out of the panic which has

been delayed for a certain time, only to occur simultaneously with the beginning of a decline of prices, and when it is thought that danger has been escaped.

As in Brussels and in the United States in 1837–1839 and in England in 1864–1866, large houses and powerful institutions of credit had maintained a whole scaffolding of speculation which was already out of plumb, but still able to stand upright through the general effect of the parts which connected them, and in this unstable equilibrium it sufficed for a single one to detach itself in order to overthrow the whole edifice at a juncture at which it was hoped it would continue to stand and even grow stronger. Does not this prove that after these epochs of expansion and activity characterizing prosperous periods (and there is no prosperous period without a rise in prices) a stoppage is necessary, a panic allowing a period of rest to permit the liquidation of transactions employed in helping to make a series of exchanges at high prices, and to allow the capital and savings of countries which had been too rapidly scattered and exhausted to reconstruct themselves during these years of tranquillity and of slackening business?

Confidence had already returned in New York despite the steady demands of the country bankers upon their correspondents, which pulled down the reserve below the legal limit; nevertheless in the midst of all the failures there was no suspension of specie payments.

The crisis of 1884, according to the Comptroller of the Currency, had been less foreseen than the crisis of 1873, and this notwithstanding it was sufficient to observe the number of enterprises and schemes flung as a prey to speculation, in order to foresee that financial troubles and disasters to the country must result.

The continuation of payments in gold, the low prices, and the outlook for a fine harvest gave courage, preserved the remaining confidence, and already allowed a speedy resumption of business to be anticipated.

The panic, although spreading over the whole Union, raged especially in New York.

Without wishing to expatiate upon its primary causes, the Comptroller of the Treasury could not help remarking that it had shown itself under the same circumstances as recently as in 1873; above all there were issues for new enterprises; the speculation had rushed to take them up at a premium, and people now asked their true value.

At this juncture railroad earnings, instead of increasing, showed weakness, and suffered a slight reaction; the solvency of houses interested began to be doubted; new loans were refused them, and immediately the artificially constructed edifice gave way.

To advance prices on the Stock Exchange, the banks had made immense loans on the shares and obligations of the new railway issues, and as soon as quotations, artificially maintained at the rates to which they had been carried, began to drop, everything became unsalable. Until this occurrence, led on and fascinated by the rise in prices, every one had bought; hardly was the advance arrested when every one reversed their operations at the same time. The bankers had loaned not only their capital but in addition a part of their clients' deposits; brokers had encouraged a speculation which brought them business; and thus it was that all hands had flung themselves upon a path that could only lead to ruin.

The Comptroller of the Currency remarks with pride that, in the midst of the general upheaval and numerous failures of honorable houses, only two National Banks were involved: one of them failed, the other suspended payment.

The amount of liability of the banks and bankers of New York who succumbed during the month of May was estimated at $32,000,000, whereas that of the only National Bank which shared their fate did not exceed $4,000,000, the bank which suspended not having occasioned any loss.

Unhappily the year did not pass without its being necessary to mention new misfortunes: eleven National Banks failed, and it is a fact that among the banks and private bankers more than a hundred were counted in the list.

Despite the close watch bestowed upon the banks it was surprising to uncover all

the tricks to which the National Marine Bank
of New York was given over, and which
until now had escaped the official examiners.

It suspended payment on May 6th, and
the same day it was debited with $555,000;
the books had been erased and overcharged
for the benefit of one client alone to the
amount of $766,000. He was a debtor to
the amount of $2,400,000, six times the
Bank's capital, and a portion of this debt
was under a good many names of subordi-
nate clerks. This same client had three
open accounts, one as administrator, then a
general account, and a special account. The
whole thing was fictitious; the schemers
sought to conceal irregularities, and had
thus imposed on the examiners and on the
Directors themselves.

The certificates issued by the clearing
house, when credit had entirely disappeared,
rendered a great service and sustained a
great number of houses in equilibrium,
which without this assistance must have
succumbed. They were granted especially
to the banks belonging to the Association,
in order to make their daily settlements.

During the crisis of 1873 the same means had been resorted to, but too late; the panic was already at its height and the commotion general, so that nothing could re-establish confidence. This was not the case in 1884: the rapidity and decision with which the Associated Banks took steps gradually re-established confidence throughout the country. The maximum of issue did not exceed $24,900,000, of which $7,000,000 were for the National Metropolitan Bank; from the 10th of June balances at the clearing house were paid in legal money. Commercial paper, which for the most part was the collateral for these certificates, had already been redeemed. The Metropolitan National Bank alone requested time to liquidate.

The issue of these certificates was very rapid: $3,800,000 on the 15th day of May, $6,800,000 on the 16th, $6,700,000 on the 17th, or more than $17,000,000 in these first three days; then on the 19th, 20th, and 22d, $1,500,000, and that was all. The remainder of the amount was given in driblets. Payments, although slower, were made from the 1st of July to the 1st of August.

Let us now run over these occurrences: in 1873 instead of $24,900,000 in certificates $26,565,000 had been issued; $22,000,000, had been issued between the 22d and the 29th of September, the redemptions took place from the 3d of November to the 31st of December.

In both cases the same amount, so to speak, had been sufficient to answer for all needs. If so small a difference sufficed to save a disordered market, people could not understand why panics could not be provided against. It was necessary to remember that this assistance was only felt when the decline of prices had already re-established an exchange of goods, bringing about the liquidation of houses unfortunately involved.

From the month of June, owing to the bank balances or the rate of exchange, the tranquillity and steadiness which had become re-established grew daily; after the storm of the first few days no new disasters had occurred except the failures of Mathew and of Morgan.

The position of the market grew firmer and the clearing house reduced its loan certificates, which now replaced the former excessive issues of bank notes. From $24,-000,000 they had already decreased to $18,000,000; of this amount $6,000,000 were taken by banks as a last resource, and there then remained only $12,000,000 in circulation. These $6,000,000 had served to sustain the shaken banks, and it is pleasant to state that outside of these requirements the amount needed was no larger.

Failures had ceased in the great centres, but they continued in the interior of the country; the shock, like a great wave, took a certain time to overrun the various States.

Succession of Panics in the United States Studied through the Balances of the Banks. —Following the historical summary of panics in the United States it will be useful to have a general table, so as to glance at the very rare documents which permit us to follow the working of the Banks through their balance sheets. We know their organization, and we take upon ourselves to state results flowing from it.

It strikes us at once that abuses and panics have constantly occurred. Can we note a difference in the frequency and gravity of the casualties, according to whether we observe them working under the former or the new (the National Bank) system, inaugurated during the War of the Secession in 1864, when the machinery for the issue of bank notes was insufficient for the new requirements?

Without lingering over the regulations before and after 1864, let us consider the differences we may ascertain by examining the balance sheets. Unfortunately, the exactness of our observation is lessened on account of the very diversity of the field it covers.

In the case of the banks of the United States we have had to content ourselves with the returns that the Comptroller of the Currency gives in his annual report on a stated day during the months of February, May, June, October, and December, beginning with the year 1865. Before

that period we had only the yearly situation of the banks of the different States
upon one given day; we are better informed on the second period; however,
basing our conclusions upon the few balance sheets we possess, we ascertain the
same series of development and increase.
Although there are lapses, still, from
another point of view, the table will
be more complete, because it embraces
all the banks of the United States. On
such an extended field, it is true, we risk
seeing great discrepancies disappear and
lose themselves in the magnitude of the
amounts whose movements we follow. In
order better to grasp them, we have put
before us the returns of the banks of the
United States, together with those of the
Associated Banks of New York City; we
may thus recognize and follow the share
played by each of them.

During the first period of the State
Banks (1811–1864), the increase in the
number of the banks was continuous, except
for two stoppages, in 1841 and in 1862;
in 1841, during the liquidation of the

panic of 1839, and in 1862 at the beginning of the War of Secession ; the crisis of
1857 did not interrupt the movement.

The capital of the banks had followed
the same changes. From $52,000,000 in
1811 to $358,000,000 in 1840, a reduction
to $196,000,000 in 1846, and finally the
last maximum reached in 1861, $429,000,-
000, at the breaking out of the war. In
1864 a new organization of the banks
under the name of " National Banks "
presented to the State Banks, without
suppressing them, a state of affairs destined to cause their liquidation, which, in
fact, practically occurred.

As in England and France, the amount
of discounts, as the balance sheets give it
to us, rose each year during the prosperous period.

Thus from 1830 to 1839 it reached
$492,000,000 from $200,000,000, to decline
again to $254,000,000 at the end of the
liquidation in 1843.

In the following period the same rising
movement from $254,000,000 to $344,000,-
000 was reproduced in 1848. The panic

in Europe burst forth in 1847; it re-
sounded very slightly in the United States
in 1848, as its subsequent liquidation in
1849 indicates, which only reduced the
local discounts to $332,000,000.

A new period of prosperity followed the
preceding events; the growing movement
re-appeared, and from $332,000,000 carried
the amount of the discounts to $684,000,-
000 between 1849 and 1857. The panic
broke out simultaneously throughout the
whole world; but notwithstanding the
wrecks it caused, such was the saving already, so healthy was the general situation
of business, that, after having thrown out
a little scum, the current of affairs resumed
its course until 1861, and discounts had already reached the amount of $696,000,000.
This amount is greater than that we have
noted in 1857, but at that time (whilst the
movement continued in Europe up to
1864), despite the shock it received by the
declaration of war here, there was complete stoppage until the end of the struggle; we have here come across a political
panic, not a business one. Peace re-estab-

lished, the movement resumed its course under new conditions and with a reorganization of the banks under the name of " National Banks." A change was due, but, as everything was made ready, it was speedy. The first balance sheet of the National Banks dates from 1864. The amount of discounts had already exceeded the sum of $100,000,000 in 1865, and grew to $500,000,000 in 1866. Once started the movement took its own course :

1865	$166,000,000	1870	$725,000,000
1866	500,000,000	1871	831,000,000
1867	609,000,000	1872	885,000,000
1868	657,000,000	1873	944,000,000
1869	686,000,000		

The yearly progression was interrupted as in Europe, and the explosion occurred at the same time. The rise in prices stopped, and incipient liquidation became apparent at the end of the year, and reduced the amount of paper on hand to $846,000,000, but, instead of lasting, as in Europe, a movement of revival, analogous to that which had followed the panic of 1864 in England, occurred. The amount of

discounts rose from $856,000,000 to $984,-
000,000 in 1875, and then, and then only,
the real retrograde movement showed itself
as in Europe, and reduced the amount of
the discounts to $814,000,000 in 1879,
simultaneously with the movement in
France and in England, when prices had
reached the lowest quotations, and when a
resumption of business was about to occur.
In a word, affairs resumed their course;
from the end of the year the amount of
paper discounted rose to $933,000,000, and
the steady advance as set forth in table
No. 3 continued each year, until it reached
$1,300,000,000 in 1884. The panic had
burst forth in Europe in 1882, and the
agitation, so lively was its impulse, lasted
during eighteen months; but, as we have
stated, the rise in prices ceased in 1882.

Starting from this time, a reaction appeared. The paper on hand lowered to
$1,200,000,000 in 1885. This liquidation
was scarcely noticeable, because we cover
the whole Union, and there is always an
upward movement in the new portions of
it which have not yet taken part in busi-

ness movements. If we note what occurred in the Associated Banks of New York, the very place where the greatest amount of business is carried on, the depression of the amount of paper on hand is most noticeable after the inflation observed at the height of the panic, while the decrease that we point out showed itself more slowly with the slackening of business. Thus, in the last period, the greatest amount of paper appears on hand—at the close of 1881, $350,000,000, and the minimum in December, 1884, the very year the panic had burst forth, and when, during the first months, the sum of $351,000,000 reappeared once more; except for a million, exactly the same amount there was in 1881.

This maximum amount was only an accident, under the influence of pressing needs at the time of the difficulty, for since 1881 the yearly reduction of the maximum and minimum amounts ensued. This tendency had occurred suddenly, and disappeared likewise; the resumption dating from 1885, a year sooner than in Europe.

The discounts of the New York Banks,

which had been reduced to $287,000,000,
rose immediately upon the opening of the
new period of prosperity, and a growing
activity carried them to $408,000,000 in
1889; after a few more fortunate years we
come to the end of the period of prosperity
and high prices.

We gather the following about discounts
from the balance sheets of the Associated
Banks of New York. If we cast our eyes
over the balance sheets of the National
Banks of the Union, we must note a falling
off of $100,000,000 in the paper discounted,
that is, from $1,300,000,000 to $1,200,000,-
000 (1884–1885). After this short period
of stoppage, clearly indicating the necessity for liquidation, discounts resumed their
steady expansion, and rose to $1,470,000,-
000 in 1886, to $1,587,000,000 in 1887, and
finally to $1,684,000,000 in 1888, when we
were in the midst of a period of development and consequently of high prices and
of prosperity; and the same is true in
France and England.

The study of a single section of the
balance sheets, that of discounts and loans,

has allowed us to follow the periods of prosperity, of panic, and of liquidation. When we next consider the other sections, we find the confirmation of our anticipations. Among these sections, in the order of importance, we notice first, public deposits in the form of running accounts; they constitute the reverse of the loans and discounts, whose total is immediately credited to the banks' clients, and the increase of paper on hand also follows. From 1865 to 1873 the steady increase was uninterrupted, viz., from $183,000,000 to $656,000,000 ; the maximum amount shows itself in the first quarter of 1873, eight months before the maximum of discounts and loans; in 1888 they ran down to $622,000,000 ; there is, say, a difference of $300,000,000 between the two totals, and this difference is the same, we observe, as that between the highest and the lowest of the two sections, as we notice it in the same year, during the liquidation of the panic of 1873.[1]

---

[1] See table of balance sheets of the Banks of the United States.

In the last period the progression is the same ; from $598,000,000 the amount of deposits advanced to $1,350,000,000, whilst discounts and loans reached $1,684,000,000 ; that is to say, there was still a difference of $334,000,000. The relationship of the two sections was much more marked than in France and in England, where the amounts carried in accounts current vary more.

In the United States we then experienced a market based on credit, which, through discounts or loans by the banks, had reached the amount of the accounts current, and was about to call the clearing house into action to settle debts every. where.

The office of the circulation of bank notes, subsequent to the severe regulations enacted in 1863 for the organization of National Banks, had varied in the last two periods that we are studying. From 1863 to 1873, after the war troubles, in propor- tion as greenbacks were withdrawn, the bank notes issued by the National Banks not only took their place, but replaced

those of the State Banks, whose position
the National Banks had taken.

We observe them rise firstly from $66,-
000,000 to $341,000,000 (1865–1873) at
the sharpest period of the panic. We might
even charge them with causing it, if the
disproportion alone of the two sums, $341,-
000,000 bank notes compared with $944,-
000,000 of bills discounted, did not at once
repel this theory. It is only necessary to
glance at this idea to see its falsity.

The maximum circulation of bank notes
has here coincided with the panic, a thing
which had not happened either in France
or in England for a long time, and instead
of presenting its highest figure during the
liquidation of the panic of 1873, it shows
us its lowest figure, $290,000,000 in 1877.
Far indeed from increasing at this time as
happened in Europe, the amount of bank
notes in circulation decreased by means of
the ebbs of metallic cash into the coffers of
the banks: in reality the cause was lacking
here; the ebb of specie was hardly felt at all.

With $4,000,000 in 1865, the reserve
was poorly provided, increasing to $48,-

000,000 in 1870. At the end of the bursting forth of the panic of 1873 it became reduced to $10,000,000, at the worst of the panic to $16,000,000 ; then, under the influence of a slight whirl, it rose to $33,-000,000 in 1874, without reaching the highest figure of the preceding period, but soon the flow reappeared and reduced this metallic reserve to $8,000,000 in 1875. It was not until after this depression that the true ebb reappeared, when the circulation of bank notes was at its lowest figure ($290,000,000).

Whilst the $8,000,000 specie reserve grew successively to $54,000,000, $79,000,-000, $109,000,000, and finally to $128,000,-000 in 1878, 1879, 1880, and 1881 ; that is to say, upon the approach of the panic, the circulation also expanded from $290,000,-000 to its highest figure $323,000,000 in 1882, the year of the European crash and of the stoppage of the rise of prices in the United States. As to the minimum amount of the specie reserve, it is to be noted in 1883, between the critical years 1882 and 1884.

Metallic reserves are too small in the United States for their fluctuations to exhibit the same regular course they offer us in Europe; the least need exhausts them, and the smallest payments fill them to overflowing. The panic soon brought about a default in payment and a need of metallic money to re-establish equilibrium, but this remedy, if it does precede panics, sometimes precedes them by a year, as we have observed in 1883, and the same irregularity is apparent whether we observe the banks of the whole United States, or the Associated Banks of the City of New York.

After the panic of 1882–1884, the ebb of specie into the coffers of the National Banks of the United States and of the Associated Banks of New York resumed its usual course, and raised its level in the case of the National Banks from $97,000,-000 to $177,000,000 between 1883 and 1885, and even to $181,000,000 in 1888. This ebb occurred both in England and France at the same time, proving that cash reserves do not increase to the detriment of each other; it is a flood of specie or of bar-gold rendered easily available, through the conclusion of the decline of prices and the slackening of business, extending to the whole world, and in which each one partakes in proportion to its wealth, and above all in proportion to its credit circulation, and of the perfection of the settlements by means of clearing houses.

This regular course in the metallic reserves is no longer to be noted in the circulation of bank notes; instead of increasing and of entering its exchanges during the return of specie into the coffers of the banks, they again took part in the paper-money reserves. From $323,000,000 in 1882 we see the circulation of bank notes decrease each year little by little until it is reduced to $151,000,000 in 1888; and this remarkable fact confronts us in the face of an unheard of expansion of business, almost 50 per cent. greater than in 1873; and of a twofold simultaneous reappearance of $84,000,000 specie and of $172,000,000 bank notes. What then is the role of specie and of bank notes in the course of business in the United States?

Much inferior to that which it plays in Europe in the absence of the machinery of a clearing house embracing the whole country, instead of being limited to some large cities.

The multiplicity of banks has strikingly helped the economic progress of the United States. From 1,500 National Banks in 1865 with a capital of $393,000,000, the number rapidly rose to 2,089 in 1876.

The panic of 1873 did not hinder the movement; however, during its liquidation, the number shrank to 2,048, only to rapidly advance to 2,500 by the close of 1882, and 2,664 in 1884, and this movement did not even suffer a slackening as in 1873 during the liquidation of its crisis; it continued steadily, and we enumerate 3,120 banks in 1888.

The increase is a third more than in 1876, but it is far from being thus in the case of the capital, which only rose from $504,000,000 to $588,000,000—that is, only 16 per cent. The small banks in the new centres of population are the factor, then, which annually increases the number.

The Condition of Business in 1888-92.[1]—
The year 1888 was fairly prosperous despite a Presidential election, but securities
were heavy, depression was general, and
some few stocks shrank amazingly. Excessive issue of new railroad securities and
disastrous competition between certain of
the Southwestern roads were without
prudence. Money was easy, bank-note
circulation continued to decrease till it was
only $151,000,000, and legal tenders to
$81,000,000, but specie reserve rose to
$181,000,000, the banking capital to $592,-
000,000 plus, the exports to $1,350,000,-
000, and discounts and loans rose to
$1,684,000,000.

The sharp speculations in wheat and the
formation of the French copper corner
caused a certain fluctuation in general business. Large crops, excepting wheat; a
flourishing cotton manufacture, a decline
in production of petroleum by agreement,
a 6 per cent. decline in pig-iron production,
a very heavy one in Bessemer iron, and a

---

[1] The facts I state in this *résumé* are based upon statistics
printed in the *Commercial and Financial Chronicle.*—DⲢC.
W. Thom.

very small export trade as compared with imports occurred. But in the year 1889, the export movement, consisting largely of cotton, was very great, being the greatest since 1880, and near the maximum, and compared favorably with the immense imports induced by the new tariff of 1890. In fact, the year 1889 surpassed all its predecessors in the volume of trade movements; the bank clearings showing an increase of 13 per cent. over 1888. The cotton, corn, and oats crops were the largest ever raised, and the wheat crop was almost the largest. But cotton brought fair prices, and cotton manufactures and production of iron were also considerably ahead of any previous year, while petroleum played an important part at good prices. Railroad earnings showed a wonderful recovery from 1888, and many reports gave the largest figures ever recorded.

During this year many consolidations and a number of foreclosures occurred. Railroad building fell to 5,000 miles compared to 7,000 in 1888. In general business, manufacturing and trade were extremely active, yielding plenty of work, good wages, and fair profits.

But the wool crop and its manufacture, a decline in the anthracite coal production, farm-mortgage pressure in the middle West, and low rates for corn and oats were untoward circumstances. Speculation on the general exchange was small, indicating a growing congestion, as was proved by the low bank reserves, especially in the last quarter of the year; but there was a heavy absorption of investment securities.

Gold, to the amount of $37,000,000, was exported in the first six months. A small amount of it returned before 1890.

Failures exceeded those of 1888 by 203 in number and about 20 per cent. in money. The woollen trade contributed much of this showing.

Importations surpassed all previous years, while exports exceeded them by nearly $20,000,000, and the net export of gold amounted to nearly $40,000,000. Money was easy during the first quarter, and then for a week a 10 per cent. rate occurred.

Thereafter, excepting the usual July 1st hardening, easy rates prevailed till August. Stiffening and fluctuating rates ensued till 30 to 40 per cent. in exceptional cases had been reached in December.

During the year, bank circulation declined to $126,000,000. Specie reserve sank to $164,000,000 and rose to $171,000,000 with the ending of the year; legal tenders to $84,000,000, and the number of banks rose to 3,326; their capital to $617,000,000; their deposits to $1,436,000,000, and their discounts and loans to $1,817,000,000, and surplus and undivided profits to $269,000,000.

Unused deposits, capital, surplus, and undivided profits were growing very small in comparison with loans and discounts at the end of the year.

The banks had to work closely, and the demands of the South and West for currency were severely felt.

Panic of 1890.—In this condition the year 1890 opened, and, with ever growing pressure for bank accommodation, displayed great activity throughout all departments of trade and transportation, with an unequalled volume of transactions.

But it was as impossible to grant to the overtrading the money needed,—though the Secretary of the Treasury, in seventy days, threw a million a day into the market by buying Government Bonds,—as it had been for the "Gentleman's Agreement" of 1888 —that of the chief railroad presidents—to maintain rates, to permanently sustain prices of railroad securities against an oversupply of them; however, both delayed the inevitable.

The debates on the silver question in Congress, leading to hopes of cheap money, and the higher prices due to this temporary and delusive stimulus; the large gross railroad earnings, demand for structural iron; the Buenos Ayres crisis, leading London to ship us large amounts of our securities; our small wheat, oats, and corn crops, and large cotton crop; the tariff discussion, ending with the McKinley Bill on October 6th, and the low bank reserves and money pressure beginning in August and lasting pretty steadily till December, and

an immense shrinking of securities, were
the chief features of the year ; and failures
beginning with that of Decker, Howell, &
Co., in New York, on November 11th, and
reaching a climax with the embarrassment
of Baring Brothers [1] in mid-November,
which failure itself greatly accelerated the
panic, were the chief events of the year.
Railroad building had increased to 6,081
miles, and the consequent new securities
were poorly absorbed.   Manufactures were
generally prosperous.

The huge imports to take advantage of

[1] Meanwhile Messrs. Charles M. Whitney & Co., David
Richmond, J. C. Walcott & Co., Mills, Roberson, & Smith,
Randall & Wierum, Gregory & Ballou, P. Gallaudet & Co., had
failed in New York, the North River Bank of that city had
been thrown into a receivership, and in Philadelphia the failure
of Messrs. Barker Brothers, had been followed by a number of
others.   This was all bad enough, but sinks into insignificance
when we recall the financial terror inspired by the great and
historic house of Baring Brothers proving unable to meet its
engagements, amounting to about £28,000,000.   The Bank of
England received notice of its difficulties on September 7th,
and by the 15th had secured from a syndicate, composed of the
great London houses, a guaranty that it would be protected
from loss to the amount of £4,000,000 if it would liquidate
the Barings' business, and from the British Government the
right to issue £7,000,000 of notes provided that sum was used
to loan the Barings, and it therefore assumed on that date the
task of paying the Barings' acceptances of £21,000,000 and

old tariff rates absorbed much money, while the Baring liquidation and that of other houses identified with South American enterprises, and the distrust bred by our Silver Bill caused a return of our securities, necessitating such a curtailment of credit that our panic took place. From July through December 31st, money ruled high and fluctuating.

The year shows a decline in circulation to $123,000,000, a decline of specie reserve to $178,000,000 with a subsequent rise to $190,000,000, a decline in legal tenders to $82,000,000, and of deposits to $1,485,-

£7,500,000 of other liabilities. Thus was averted what would probably have been the greatest panic in the world's history. That which occurred was a mere bagatelle to what was threatened. It is difficult to bestow too much credit upon Mr. William Lidderdale, Governor of the Bank of England, for conceiving and managing this plan. He has saved hundreds of thousands of homes and interests from misery. Under his able administration it is expected to extinguish the Barings' liabilities without calling on the Government, and it is believed something will be saved for the Barings from their former assets in business. This is deeply to be wished, for though the Barings have continued business under form of a stock concern with a million pounds capital, they are wonderfully restricted as compared with their former state. They have performed in banking too many helpful actions in furtherance of civilization to be eclipsed without sincere regret.

000,000, while the banks increased to 3,573 with a capital of $657,000,000, and a surplus and reserve of $316,000,000, and discounts and loans rose to $1,932,000,000.

The year 1891 has exhibited the usual incidents succeeding a time of reorganizations after panics and, after a period of selling and settlement, a rehabilitation of affairs and the consequent advance in prices of securities. The unprecedented abundance of our crops as a whole, coupled with the almost universal shortage in European countries, largely aided the rehabilitation. Bank balances reflected this startlingly. On February 26, 1891, loans and discounts and over-drafts amounted to $1,927,654,-559.80. On May 4, 1891, loans and discounts and over-drafts amounted to $1,969,-$46,379.67. On the former date capital, deposits, surplus, and undivided profits amounted to $2,462,456,677.92, and on the latter date to $2,567,288,143.45.

On July 9, 1891, discounts, loans, and over-drafts amounted to $1,963,704,948.07, and capital, deposits, surplus, and undivided profits to $2,522,609,679.78.

Confidence is restored and prices have advanced, and should advance still further. There seem to be only three things that could check the advancing market, and of those the two chief ones seem pretty surely relegated to a fairly distant future. These latter two are, in the order of importance: (1) a free silver law, *i.e.*, a law making, say, 67 cents' worth of silver pass for an equivalent of a 100-cent dollar; and (2) a very radical and abrupt change in our tariff law. The remaining and very minor influence is the breaking out of a general European war, which would at first induce a selling of our securities, and so lower prices, but which finally and shortly would benefit us by a subsequent returning flood of money exchanged for our various bread-stuffs, and supplies, and even securities of different sorts.

It would be better for our future if the liquidation of the last panic had been more radical in some cases, notably in land speculation. In this liquidation has not been thorough, and, as far as these cases influence the market, it has remained for a long time unsound, and even now is not fully re-covered.

The past twelve months have witnessed a continued settling of old accounts, and the undertaking of new business, in a limited way, despite a somewhat uneasy feeling about silver and the now accomplished Presidential election. But the fact that an analysis of the bank returns to the Comptroller of the Treasury shows that available. resources (capital, deposits, surplus, and undivided profits), as compared with demands (loans and discounts), are good and growing, considered in regard to the other signs indicating prosperity (see Introduction), justifies the prediction of the steady development of a prosperous period.

Panic of 1893-4.—It was early in 1893 that I wrote the last page of *A Brief History of Panics in the United States.* Two of the three checks to business prosperity to which I then referred, virtually occurred very soon. The determined resolve of the "free silver" members of Congress to continue the heavy monthly utterance of silver dollars redeemable at par in gold kept many business men most disquieted. They saw that the free gold in the Treasury was sinking greatly and steadily. They knew, also, that there was semi-official assertion of the right of the United States to redeem its silver dollars in Government notes. The Free-Coinage Bill had been passed by the Senate in July. The House defeated it. The legal fights against certain great railroad combinations and frequent labor strikes put additional burdens on the market.

In the United States and abroad the doubt of our willingness and ability to redeem our obligations at par in gold on demand grew most rapidly. Accordingly, exports of gold increased and hoarding of it began at home. To all this was added the expectation of a severe downward revision of our tariff laws if the Democratic Party should succeed, as was expected, in the Presidential election in November.

Business was scared and slowing down and, therefore, using less and less of its working capital. The false ease of increasing loanable funds in the custody of the banks lulled many into a specious confidence. But gold was exported in increasing quantities. Should the Government issue bonds in exchange for gold for the purposes of redemption? The Philadelphia & Reading receivership occurred. Easy money led to many consolidations of transportation properties and to very many large commitments. Money tightened. In March, it loaned at 60% per annum. Would President Cleveland call an extra session of Congress in March to repeal the silver law and to issue bonds in order to replenish the free gold in the Treasury? The

Stock Market showed a great decline in quotations.

In April, 1894, Secretary of the Treasury Jno. G. Carlisle forbade the further issuance of gold certificates for gold deposited in the Treasury under Act of July 12, 1882, whenever the gold in the Treasury "reserved for the redemption of United States notes falls below $100,000,000." This further alarmed the business world, which was not reassured when on the 20th Carlisle announced that the Treasury would pay gold for all Treasury notes so long as he had "gold lawfully available for that purpose." President Cleveland, that stalwart man, uttered this high and firm pronouncement on April 24th: "The President and his Cabinet are absolutely harmonious in the determination to exercise every power conferred upon them to maintain the public credit, to keep the public faith, and to preserve the parity between gold and silver and between all financial obligations of the Government." Very good, thought business, but how and when will you act accordingly?

Lack of business confidence increased greatly. Money rates advanced. Security values fell; imports greatly exceeded exports. Silver certificates were at 83. Something was about to snap in the general business machine. National Cordage broke from 57 to 15½ on May 1st, receivers were appointed, and the panic of 1894 had declared itself and grew worse on the 4th and 5th. Call money rose to 40%. June witnessed great distress in business circles. On the 27th the Government of India stopped the coinage of silver for individuals and decreed the exchange value of the rupee at 16 pence. This lowered the exchange value of our silver bullion certificates to 62. President Cleveland helped matters somewhat by announcing that Congress would be convened early in September. In early July the panic increased somewhat despite the President's call for Congress to assemble on August 7th. Time loans were hardly obtainable. Conditions in August grew worse. Business was almost at a standstill, and failures were very frequent. From August 7th until the affirmative action on the 28th by the House of Representatives as to the repeal of the Silver Act, there was great concern.

Then hope revived; but hoarding of currency increased. Great banking interests in New York helped the situation mightily by importing over $40,000,000 gold. September was an anxious but more hopeful month as the prompt adoption by the Senate of the Free-Silver Bill was anticipated. However, the weary debate dragged on in the Senate. President Cleveland demanded the unconditional adoption of the House measure. Certain compromisers, led by Senator Arthur P. Gorman of Maryland, suggested that during each of the following fifteen months the Government purchase the minimum amount of 1,000,000 ounces of silver, and then stop all such purchases against which silver certificates had to be issued. This plan for speedy action President Cleveland and the Secretary of the Treasury opposed as worthless unless concurrently there was

an issue of $100,000,000 of Government
bonds to replenish the gold in the Treasury. They asserted that new legislation
must be had before any such bonds could
be validated. So the business world continued to suffer.

Let me here state the fact, that without
any fresh authorization, Secretary of the
Treasury Carlisle did in January, 1895,
issue $50,000,000 of Government bonds
to replenish the free gold in the Treasury,
and that an injunction suit against their
sale was dissolved by Judge Cox at
Washington on the 30th of that month.
Gorman had been right. The credit of
the country would not have suffered by
the additional issuance of some final
$60,000,000 (?) of silver certificates if the
gold in the Treasury had concurrently
been upbuilt to the extent of $50,000,000
to $100,000,000; but an immensity of
business loss would have been averted.

But to resume the orderly recital of
those times. October dragged along its
weary length, while the Senate debated
and business withered. Finally, on the

30th, the Senate accepted unconditional repeal of the Free-Silver Act. On November 1st, it became a law. The fear of repudiation thus escaped, though with fearful loss, the country plunged into all the unsettlement caused by a too sudden and too extensive change in the tariff. These changes were announced by the House Committee on December 27th.

The conditions mentioned in the last paragraph beginning on page 22 of the introduction to this book, were at work. Before the market had recovered from the "Silver panic" of 1893-4, the terror caused to the business world by the proposed very decided changes in the customs dues laid hold upon every trader in the United States and reflectedly upon every one of its citizens. It shook business throughout. Would not such a plan as is set forth in the footnote below[1]

[1] " Mr. DeCourcy W. Thom expressed himself yesterday as heartily indorsing the Democratic celebration to be held in this city January 17 next, to which all the party leaders will be invited and at which subjects of interest to the party will be discussed.

have virtually prevented all that?   When
I sent that plan, which I had stated in an
interview in the *Baltimore Sun* of December 24, 1910, to the various members of
the Finance Committee of the United

" When asked to give his opinion on some of the questions
worthy of discussion at this gathering Mr. Thom mentioned
the tariff and economy in the conduct of national affairs.

" In the coming national Democratic celebration," he said,
" I hope suggestions dealing with a rational reformation of
the tariff and the need for national economy of every kind
will be duly considered, and that on these two subjects alone,
to be treated thoroughly but temperately, will this national
Democratic gathering advise our party as to its best course to
pursue.

" In three successive Presidential canvasses since the Civil
War the Democratic party has received a majority vote of the
people of the United States, and in my opinion would have
gained three thereby, instead of the alternate two, elections to
the Presidency if the tariff issue, the major one of the two
great issues—namely, tariff and economy—on which they won,
had been so sought to be applied as not to threaten unduly to
affect general business."

PROTESTS AGAINST EXTRAVAGANCE

" All will agree with me that a reasonable economy, instead of the actual wild extravagance of government, is more
than ever a national need.   Who will disagree with me, that
in addition to the contribution from internal revenue, the
tariff should be used merely to contribute towards the due
expenses of the Government economically administered, but
so applied as not to break down the standard of American
citizenship, as exemplified in the working people of our

States Senate and to the Committee on Ways and Means of the House of Representatives, very many of them wrote me affirmatively on the subject.

To revert, however to the due order

---

country; and eked out, if it is possible, by contributions into the national treasury of sound inheritance taxes ? "

URGES CUT ON NECESSARIES

" Is it not possible to apply that general plan as follows : Divide, say, all of the articles now upon the tariff list into three classes.

" (*a*) All such as are usually found in the typical American homes—I mean the homes of those admirably called by Grover Cleveland the 'plain people,' who are just the same class, I believe, as those indicated by Abraham Lincoln, when he said, 'God must greatly love the common people, for he made so many of them '—and put that list of articles on a free list or a severely tariff-for-revenue-only list.

" (*b*) Create a second division composed of all the articles of luxury. Put upon them the very highest tariff they will stand and yet come into the country, except in the case of articles of antique art. These latter should be admitted free.

" (*c*) Keep upon all other articles now in the tariff list the actual duties for the period of one year, but after that period and the actual imposition of the proposed new tariff I am discussing shall have begun, put all the articles involved in Class *c* upon a tariff-for-revenue-only basis, so constructed as not to break down the standard of the American workingman's living."

YEAR TO MARKET STOCK

" This period of one year—say, would allow manufacturers to market their stock on hand or already required to be pro-

of our tale. It was on January 17,
1895, that Secretary of the Treasury
John G. Carlisle, without any new legislative authority, offered to sell $50,000,000
Government bonds already mentioned.

---

duced on the basis of the market influenced by the quasi-
Government protection extended by the existing tax laws of
the nation.

" At the end of this period the manufacturer would be
obliged to produce at less cost in order to find a market in
competition with his foreign competitor, which competition
would result in lower prices that he and his foreign competitors
would have to offer to the working people and other citizens
of our country."

EFFECT ON WAGES

" Those working people and other citizens would for a year
have been enjoying at lesser cost all of the articles used in
the typical American home I have referred to and could without loss therefore well afford to submit to a reduction in wages
so long as that reduction in wages was contemporaneous with
affording them a proportionate or more than proportionate
reduction in cost of the articles for whose purchase those
wages were sought to be expended. At the same time, the
manufacturer at a proportionately lesser cost of production,
through this reduction in wage-paying, would be selling as
much or more of his old products at their old profit.

" Could we add to the income from the tariff and internal
revenue the sums derived from the sound national inheritance
tax I have mentioned above it is evident we would have sup-
plied for the period of change from one tax system to another
an ' adequate governor' to use a mechanical illustration, to
prevent undue oscillation of prices in the business world."

If issued during the Silver-repeal fight when Gorman proposed his compromise, and if Carlisle had made it clear very early that as many such issues for gold would be made as were needed to keep the trading public safeguarded against any monetary-business cramping caused by the governmental policy affecting the tariff, a minimum rather than something approaching a maximum of disturbance would have followed. In better spirits because of the issuance of the $50,000,000 Government bonds for gold, the business

---

BANK RESOURCES TO PREVENT STRAIN

" The further use of the existing financial agencies for co-operation of the banks in all sections to mass resources and apply them to prevent undue local strain upon credit dispels the fear of any necessary injury to the financial fabric in effecting this change.

" Grover Cleveland, whose character and principles I have long revered, seemed to me in the application of his plan for tariff reform to have endangered at once the success and the permanence of his reform of the tariff—which you recall was confessedly and very properly not a reformation to free trade—by failing to provide in it a method for avoiding or at least minimizing and shortening any incident disturbance to the business world. His plans, further, failed by not reasonably insuring for the transition period from the old tariff to the new one sufficient national income for national expenses."

world worked along. The House had
passed the Tariff Bill early in February
by a big majority. Business soon looked
up decidedly. But the Seigniorage Bill
was adopted in March. President Cleveland, that sturdy upholder of the Nation's credit, vetoed it. He knew that
any new moral obligation to keep at a
parity with gold dollars worth in themselves less than one hundred cents in
gold would materially shake domestic
and foreign credit.

The veto had a deservedly splendid
effect upon all our trading interests.
This was increased by the failure of the
House to override the President's veto
of the Seigniorage Bill. But the Senate
had not acted on the Tariff Bill. Business dwindled and there occurred strikes
and other widespread labor troubles,
especially in the bituminous coal trade.
In many parts of the country the militia,
and in Chicago United States troops, had
to be employed to maintain order. Call
money was a drug on the market. The
net gold in the Treasury was very low.

The Tariff Bill dragged its weary length along. President Cleveland and Chairman William L. Wilson of the Ways and Means Committee of the House insisted that the bill would produce sufficient revenue for the expenses of the Government. Senator Gorman and others in the United States Senate insisted to the contrary and demanded that the tariff on sugar should be kept at a high figure. A bitter controversy ensued. Finally, on August 13th, the House accepted the Senate Tariff Bill. It was time for some affirmative action, for among other threatening conditions the net gold in the Treasury had fallen to the lowest figure since resumption of specie payments in 1879.

Business began to revive. The issue of $50,000,000 Government bonds for gold to replenish the Treasury stock was a very stimulating influence. The improvement dated virtually from the agreement in February between the Government and the Morgan-Belmont Syndicate to prevent the export of gold. In June,

1895, the Government gold was thus
brought up to a round $100,000,000 for
the first time since December, 1894. But
notwithstanding the fact that the business
outlook was decidedly better, the inevitable disturbances to business following
a general change in the tariff, unsettled
political conditions in Europe and the
selling of American securities owned
abroad, the shortage of the American
cotton crop, President Cleveland's Vene-
zuela message, which many persons
thought might bring on war with England,
and another decline in the Treasury
free gold, again shook business confidence.

Improvement, however, was stimulated by a remarkable increase in the
supply of money in our balance of trade
and by the virtual settlement of the
Venezuelan question. The business situation was steadily clearing. The ills from
the panic of 1893–4 were well behind us.
The Spanish-American war proved to
be harmless to us financially, while it
tended to show that National neighborli-

ness could be exercised in a splendidly
unselfish way. By our treaty of peace
with Spain on December 10, 1898, an
additional emphasis was given to the
revival of trade. During 1899 a great
rush to speculate brought the pinches
in money inevitable in those pre-Reserve
Bank days, but could not stop the general
broadening of business interests although
the industrial situation was unsatis-
factory in spots. Indeed, the succeeding
year was to witness severe industrial
trouble destined to cause a general set-
back in business. The situation cleared
considerably when the November elections of 1900 showed the country to be
safe from the Bryan silver policy.

Big business interests took hold of
market conditions. Huge combinations
of trade interests became the order of
the day. The United States Steel trust
was the vastest and was the transcendent
achievement of J. Pierpont Morgan.
The Stock Exchange was wild with speculation. The collapse came there in the
famous decline of the 9th of May, 1901,

precipitated by the Northern Pacific corner. In a month the market was tranquil again. The shooting of President McKinley produced great financial nervousness. The over-trading abroad, especially in Germany, was influencing us and all the rest of the world, which had not yet recovered from the vast financial cost of the English Boer War.

The ever increasing closeness of business relations the world over — their virtual solidarity, in fact—was being illustrated again with us. A chief example was trouble in the copper groups following a slackened world demand for their products.

Overtrading was doing its usual work. This induced loss of business courage in many quarters, or shall I say a realization that nowhere in the American business system was there any arrangement empowered so to marshal the competent strength of financial America that large and overwhelming disturbances should become impossible in business generally. Indeed, the Government forces seemed to tend contrariwise to big business practices. They took virtually their first step in "trust-busting" when they tried to break up the Northern Securities Company, which had been concocted to handle the celebrated Northern Pacific case. Labor troubles supervened. Many great speculative stock campaigns collapsed. The banks yielded to the imperative need to reduce credits. The year 1902 had almost experienced a widespread panic: but the marshaling of great private resources had restored confidence temporarily, and it closed in peace.

Panic of 1903.—Then came the real beginning of the protracted "trust busting" campaign. Business took fright, for it believed it was to be bullied rather than soundly regulated. Great failures on the Stock Exchange were its sure indications. Fear and distrust was upon all the American business world. Industries languished. Money was easy because less and less employed in trade. The great captains of industrial finance, however, patched up troubles and differ-

ences here and there and, availing themselves of the plentiful supply of money,
soon had a notable speculation at work.
Gradually the country took heart again
and business experienced a revival.

It was thought that President Roosevelt, elected in November, 1904, would
help bring about discrimination between
"good" trusts and "bad" trusts, and
whose "trust" is bad! But "trust busting" became an even more popular and
political pursuit. Indeed, the abuses prac-
tised by many of them had created a
situation regarding which the question
was becoming in the popular mind simply
this, "Shall trustdom rule the people or
the people rule the trusts?" The sound
control of both before the Constitution
of their country must be the happy
solution.

The Bill of May 9th of the House of
Representatives, giving the Interstate
Commerce Commission power to fix
railroad rates, was ominous, and little
noticed by the general business world; but
some noticed and acted. The Senate

had not voted; nor did they realize what
rate-regulation implied to railroad balance
sheets and so to the Stock Exchange.
Some interest was selling securities. The
business public was awakening to the
fact that legislators, legislation, the people,
and the law were hot after the business
methods of many organizers. Fear,
founded on a tardy awakening to facts,
declared itself, but spasmodically, for
now and again the great captains of
finance and industry were trying to save
the situation. They successfully aided
whatever of momentum there was in
general business. But Congressional activity as to any combinations in restraint
of trade was unabated. It called upon
the President for such information as the
Interstate Commerce Commission might
have as to a combination in restraint of
trade between the Pennsylvania Railroad
and certain lines allied with it.

The battle between the old style and
the new style of managing great corporations was fairly on. Labor troubles
added to the existing disarrangement of

business. San Francisco's vast earthquake and consuming fire sucked much capital away from financial centres in order to replace the $350,000,000 of capital destroyed. The money market was greatly restricted. The stock market showed signs of panic. The Secretary of the Treasury continued to help the situation as best he knew how. Notably, he offered $30,000,000 Panama Canal Bonds, and very successfully sold them. That afforded an additional basis for bank-note issuing. The stock market responded with a fine upward swing. Heavy dividends were declared by certain leading railroad and other corporations. Indeed many high records were made by securities and so distracted attention from that steady tide of keener inspection and stricter regulation by the agents of the people which was destined to unmoor and toss and injure many a financial craft. Railroads asserted that the country needed a great increase in railroad trackage, but that the actual treatment of the roads deterred extensions through frightening capital. So the year 1906 wore away after having sorely tried the nerves of the whole business world which it left in a most justly apprehensive state.

The Panic of 1907.—The panic of 1907 opened with great but feverish activity in business. Driven by necessity the railroads adopted the issuance of short-time notes for new capital, as the market would absorb no long-time obligations except at forbidding interest rates. Any signally untoward happening could promptly precipitate a panic. The United States Treasury withdrawal of Government deposits from the banks, and the collapse of the Knickerbocker Trust Company in New York were such happenings.

On March 14th, the panic declared itself and pandemonium ruled on the New York Stock Exchange,—that prominent barometer of business conditions. In its coming it had exemplified again the characteristic symptoms of a panic which I have set forth on pages 7–16 of the introduction to this book. After the spasm of March 14th and the business cataclysm of the following October, the business world staggered along, but with the strength merely that results from courage and the exercise of reserve power husbanding its resources and lightening its load. The decrescendo movement of another business cycle had begun. Runs on financial institutions were prominent in our country. But throughout all the western world resources were strained. Money had been overused. Money rates were extremely high. Failures were frequent everywhere. In our own country painful disturbances, relaxation, and unrest were everywhere apparent. The radical doctrines of many political leaders tended to further unrest.

The business of the country was halting between the need sanely to regulate "big business" and the fact that "big business" had been obliged to fight for prosperity in the welter of unallowable but very often undeniable conditions. The railroads justly claimed that they were forbidden living rates. Their opponents accused them of carelessness and waste. The railroads and the Interstate Commerce Commission were the protagonists respectively of the conservative and the radical thought of the country, which is so rich in natural wealth and is inhabited by so resourceful a people that though by statutes they be well managed or not, their National wealth increases. So ran the business world away, but with a very slow and steady approach towards a rational rectification of disputed legislation as affecting business. Meanwhile the courageous "captains of industry" were leading in business as best they could and were better appreciating the temper and needs of the American people.

Added to the difficulties resulting from our languishing trade at home, we suffered reflectedly from the constriction of business in Europe, which was acutely aware that the disturbance in the Balkans threatened to destroy the peace of Europe. Conditions were not yet quite ready there for a cataclysmic war. For example, statistics had not quite demonstrated to Germany that the physique of her people and the rate of increase of their families were declining while the expenditures for superpreparedness for war was demanding either retroaction in that regard or else an expenditure from the principal of their property. Germany did make in one year the sacrifice of five per cent. of her principal for yet fuller preparedness for war. Indeed since late in 1908, it is fair to say that consciously or unconsciously the whole world has been in travail. Whatever broad measures statesmen anywhere have promulgated, have been subjected to the unusual stress and strain of world-wide unrest. Like the treacherous undertow that wrenches those who venture in, has been the world unrest upon all phases, incidences, and predicates of business. Some of us have long realized this; some have not.

With November, 1908, came the election of that great constitutionist, Taft, to the American Presidency upon a platform less radical than that of his opponent. This heartened the constructive forces of the country. But very little upbuilding resulted. The coming revision of the tariff was of itself sufficient further to restrict business undertakings, and to cause many great producers of goods to arrange to unload at lowering prices their actual and their future outputs. But the conserving of resources since the panic had helped the superficial situation, and the spasmodic stimulus that so often follows a general heightening of the tariff showed itself after the adoption of the tariff bill in August, 1909.

The illness and after a month or two the death of the great business leader, Harriman, caused in the securities market a great decline. Fundamental conditions were unsettled. The best that could be expected was a see-saw movement until some power should set our country and the business world at large once more securely on their respective bases. The Anti-Trust Law, the Interstate Commerce Law, and such like influences continued to disturb the United States, while Europe was beneath the surface unendingly agitated.

General business marked time while statesmen or pseudo-statesmen planned and promised panaceas. President Taft joined that populous group. The securities market, that barometer of business, fell beneath such assurance of further unsettlement. How can you continue to trade unless reasonably sure that conditions will remain fairly constant! All this militated against a normally quick recovery from a great panic. Little scares were frequently experienced. Influences matured and presented one great political party split into two great factions, while the other chief party endured something of the same development.

A conservative handling of National policies, or a radical one was the question in each case. The November elections indicated a popular revolt against the party in power—the Republican. Unshaken, President Taft followed his con-

victions and in his Presidential message,
of December, 1910, to Congress called
for a halt in legislating to regulate corporations, until the effect of the laws on
the statute books could be studied. The
stock, money, and industrial markets
were marking time. Not to go forward
in business or elsewhere is in itself to
retrograde. Thus opened the year 1911.
Under the influence of easy money,
better business on some of the western
railroads, better dividend declarations
here and there, a rosy prediction as
to the early future of the iron market,
and the belief that the Interstate Commerce Commission would grant better
rates to the railroads, general business
felt encouraged and prices advanced
somewhat. But in February the Interstate Commerce Commission forbade the
railroads any increase whatever in rates.
The roads were obliged to institute many
cramping economies which to them very
often meant the using up of their corpus
and to the business world of the United
States a permeating retrogressive influ-

ence.   Reductions in railroad dividends were symptomatic of that. To add to all this there developed additional business unrest predicated in the general tariff change favored by the House of Representatives in April.

The United States Supreme Court decision interpreting the Sherman Anti-Trust Law of 1890 as affecting the Standard Oil Company case and the American Tobacco Company case were delivered late in May and were unexpectedly reassuring to business. This was another evidence that the best thought of the Nation everywhere was seeking to rectify the looseness of the past without killing business initiative and continued endeavor. So matters see-sawed in the business world. It was indeed in a state of unstable equilibrum. Stocks declined now abruptly; then, after some slight recovery, gently; but the slant was decidedly downward.

The Government felt that its duty required it to push forward the investigation of industrial corporations; and that the Nation so demanded. And it was in October that the chief of such corporations—the United States Steel Trust—had a Government suit for dissolution filed against it. The sturdy bell-wether of the corporation flock was attacked by the great United States Government. What would happen to the humbler members of the flock! Certain court decisions were reassuring to corporations in November and business brightened for the time being and during much of December in certain notable instances, for in that month the Interstate Commerce Commission report appeared and seemed less drastic in tone.

The year 1912 opened with an additional influence promising increased alarm and marking of time. I mean that candidates for the Presidential nomination began their canvasses, which, of course, implied new plans for making new laws to govern business conditions. Former President Roosevelt announced his candidacy in February. President Taft was already constructively in the field.

Governor Harmon of Ohio was mentioned
in many quarters as a successful reformer
who wished soundly to guide but not
unwittingly injure business, while Under-
wood was similarly praised in addition to
his record on the recasting of the tariff
into a further revenue measure. Champ
Clark, Speaker of the House of Representatives, was a popular candidate.
And Woodrow Wilson loomed up as
though forecast by destiny. At first
and in many important sections of the
country considerably more delegates to
the Republican National Presidential Con-
vention were chosen for Mr. Taft than
for Mr. Roosevelt. This and brisker
business served to hearten conservative
interests, and the general market revived
despite the decidedly downward influence
in our country of the gigantic strike
among English coal operators, who thereby spread trouble throughout the British
Empire, and, through the solidarity of
the financial world to-day, affected every
financial centre.

The remainder of the year was dominated by the Presidential canvass. Taft, called by many a "stand-patter"; Roosevelt, "the insurgent," who proposed to mend all the troubles of the political public by his usual brusque methods; and Woodrow Wilson, the "conservative with a move on," made their appeals for popular support. Until the verdict in November a see-saw market took place in the United States, while Europe and reflectedly the remainder of the world became alarmed lest the war declared in October by the Balkan States against Turkey should produce world-wide trouble.

The November Presidential election showed that Woodrow Wilson received 435 votes, Mr. Roosevelt 90, and Mr. Taft 8. However, the popular vote for Woodrow Wilson was more than 1,000,000 below that cast for Messrs. Roosevelt and Taft jointly, and about 2,000,000 short of a majority of all the votes cast for the Presidential nominees—Socialist, Republican, Democratic, and so on. But the vitally significant fact is that the popular vote for the "stand-pat" candidate—

Mr. Taft—was very small in comparison with the joint vote of the three candidates whose platforms called for a drastic handling of National policies,—Debs, Roosevelt, and Wilson.

Drastic recasting of the rules of any game unsettles play. The market dropped. But fortunately for the country the ripe and balanced and active intellect and character of Woodrow Wilson, elected President, lent much re-assurance against the extensive political surgery he had been chosen to perform. All knew that he would be thorough and reasoning. All the grievous handicaps that business suffers from uncertainty of regulation, it was thought would be overcome as promptly as possible. But the pledged great change of the tariff was enough to induce retrenchment of business endeavor. With a major factor unusual in any proposition, how can stability, much less progress, be expected in any interest?

The Panic of 1913.—Retrogression in business began very early in 1913 and increased until mid-October, 1914. On October 3, 1913, the new Tariff had become a law; but other reforms still jostled business. However, by mid-October, 1914, the Interstate Commerce Commission seemed to have become less radical in its views, the Industrial Trade Commission was at work apparently studying the essentials of the industrial situation, the United States Supreme Court was delivering opinions in check of indeterminate statutory meddling with business and the splendid potential of the Reserve Bank system was offering for use.

It is hard not to overstate the vast re-assurance offered to business by linking together the banking power of the country through the Reserve Bank system. Just as an enormously large number of troops skilfully thrown into an endangered—a panicky—position will ensure success, so can the vast resources of the Reserve Bank system restore financial order when panic fear is declaring itself. During the past two years of threatening from the disturbances in Mexico, our country has learned to forecast the benefit that the Reserve Bank system predicates; but our stay and confidence has been the cool and far-seeing statesmanship of our great President, Woodrow Wilson.

The breaking out of the "World War" in August, 1914, had so flooded our market with securities held in Europe that the Stock Exchange, following the continental example, closed from July 31st till November 28th, when the New York Stock Exchange and other American stock exchanges opened for restricted business in bonds and on December 15th to unlimited trading in stocks and bonds. Other kinds of exchanges acted much the same. This checked business in every direction, despite the great issuance of temporary Clearing House certificates. In two months the latter tendency was changed in many quarters.

Then began the "war boom." Gradually it has spread, bringing such enormous profits in all our lines of business supplying the needs of the "Great War," that the first twelve months of it showed more than a billion dollars trade balance in our favor, and that balance then began increasing on a progressive scale. Money is yet plentiful. All business is stimulated. Our crops are unexampled in quantity and money value. Everything points to great prosperity unchecked until the "Great War" ceases and withdraws the stimulating demand for our supplies.

Then will come a readjustment of our trade. Money will have become actually or potentially scarce because of the previous vast expansion of our business, and all the banking power of our country will be requisite to prevent a crashing panic. The Reserve Banks will have gotten fully to work by then, it is to be hoped. They will be needed to lead in the life-saving operations. Such first aid to the injured will obviate such financial sufferings as the old-time panics presented. They can hardly be expected to reduce the casualties to the volume of the slow panic in securities in the year 1913, for the volume of business involved at present is vastly more swollen and the kind more circumscribed.

It is interesting to note that panics have continued to appear about as regularly as usual, but less crushingly, since 1890, the date up to which the first and second editions of this book had traced them. Remedial or partially preventive measures have been more and more utilized by the financial powers to control them. Never will panics cease so long as trade and fear are exemplified on this earth, but just as modern medicine is overcoming the dangers threatening the physical man, so is modern finance overcoming panic and the other dangers which threaten financial stability. After all, reserve power and only a rational use of financial resources are the surest preventive of panic. And that the American people have not been forced through entrance into the "World War" to deplete their reserve strength, especially in a financial way, is due to the splendid conduct of our great President. He is leading this country to unexampled prosperity. Instead of consenting that old abuses in the business world should continue until an over-indignant public had grown riotously injurious, he has guided the current of their wrath, initiated or promulgated the methods for redressing their grievances, and has saved to the country, to its people, and to general business itself, the splendid and full service of business enterprise freed from the abuses and handicaps that unregulated conditions had forced it to employ in the unrestrained struggles of the open mart.

DeCourcy W. Thom.

INDEX

Matthew 5:1–2

And seeing the multitudes, He went up on a mountain, and when He was seated His disciples came to Him. Then He opened His mouth and taught them.

Matthew 5:3

Blessed are the poor in spirit,
For theirs is the kingdom of heaven.

Matthew 5:4

Blessed are those who mourn,
For they shall be comforted.

Matthew 5:5
    Blessed are the meek,
      For they shall inherit the earth.

Matthew 5:6
    Blessed are those who hunger and thirst for righteousness,
    For they shall be filled.

Matthew 5:7
    Blessed are the merciful,
      For they shall obtain mercy.

THE
BIBLE
VERSE
BOOK

THE
BIBLE
VERSE
BOOK

LaVonne Masters

THOMAS NELSON PUBLISHERS
Nashville

Published in Nashville, Tennessee, by Thomas Nelson,
Inc., and distributed in Canada by Lawson Falle, Ltd.,
Cambridge, Ontario.

Printed in the United States of America.

Scripture quotations are from the NEW KING JAMES
VERSION of the Bible. Copyright © 1979, 1980, 1982,
Thomas Nelson Publishers, Inc.

Library of Congress Cataloging-in-Publication Data

Masters, LaVonne.
     The Bible verse book / LaVonne Masters.
          p.   cm.
     Summary: Presents five steps to help children
memorize the Scriptures and understand and apply
those verses to their lives at home, at school, and
with their friends.
     ISBN 0-8407-3229-5
     1. Bible—Memorizing.   2. Christian education of
children.
[1. Bible—Memorizing.   2. Christian life.] I. Title.
BS617.7.M37   1991
220′.07—dc20   91-7606
                                                          CIP
                                                          AC

Printed in the United States of America
1 2 3 4 5 6 7 — 96 95 94 93 92 91

To my cherished grandchildren

Jonathan David and Christie LaVonne Westerfield.

Special acknowledgment to

Kathy Dawson
for her skills in children's education
that made this edition possible.

Thank you.

CONTENTS

A NOTE TO PARENTS

I have had parents say to me numerous times, "I don't want to make my children rebellious by forcing them to attend church or making them read the Bible." However, when they are encouraged with the right spirit, I've never seen children become rebellious about going to church or learning the Word. It is the child who does not learn faithfulness in church attendance and a love for the Scriptures who has no foundation of values and will, in the end, become rebellious.

As parents, we want the very best for our children. We send them to school to learn. We teach our children habits for health and cleanliness. We do anything we can to help them become involved in the extracurricular activities of their choice: music, sports, hobbies, travel, computers.

The best way to guide our children spiritually is to live the way we expect our children to live. The best way to help our children learn to memorize and meditate on Scripture is for us to memorize and meditate on Scripture. If we are learning the teachings and principles with Scripture through Memorize and Meditate, and if we are consistently practicing these in our lives, our children will not depart from our spiritual training and will grow up to respect and revere us and the God we serve.

You will find the complete memorization and meditation program for adults in my book for adults, *Memorize and Meditate*. As you work through the five D's of the program—decide the method, determine the location, discover the content, draw the application, and do it—you can be available to help your children walk through the steps of the program. Learning the Scriptures as a family also gives the entire family an opportunity to better understand and encourage one another. Take time once a week to give each member of the family an opportunity to share what he is learning. Saturday nights or Sunday evenings are good times for this.

Take time to read through this book with your children, or at least to read it before they use it. Before your children begin to learn and use the five D's of Memorize and Meditate, help them choose a Bible translation that is appropriate for their age, yet try to choose one they will not quickly outgrow. The five D's for Kids' Memorize and Meditate are the same as the five D's for the adults' program.

Decide the Method

Help your children choose the one method of memorization they are most comfortable with. Remember, memorizing is easy for kids. Their minds are fresh and quick. And the most common way children learn information and facts is by repetition. So this should be a guaranteed method of learning. However, the other methods are equally as valid, and sometimes very helpful.

Two methods of memorization that are especially helpful for younger children are association and the use of cassette tapes. Association involves relating each verse to a picture you or your child draws. Keep the picture simple.

For children who enjoy listening to cassettes, record portions of Scripture so they can listen to the tapes throughout the day. The children will not only learn Scripture but they will have the reassurance of hearing Mom or Dad's voice during the day. And if they play the Scripture tapes just before they go to sleep at night, they'll sleep better.

Determine the Location

You may want to help your children determine the portion of Scripture they memorize. I've included two lists of passages: one in chapter 4, pages 49–50, and one, which is arranged according to age, at the back of the book. It is less work for you if all your children are working on the same Scriptures at the same time. However, one child may need a different Scripture because of his or her specific need for encouragement or instruction, or because he or she is not at the same level as the other children. Be sensitive to this and help each child determine the number of verses he or she can comfortably memorize each week.

Discover the Content

When researching key words with preschoolers, you may not want to use a dictionary. Instead, use examples to teach word meanings. To teach the meaning for the word *kind*, for example, you might demonstrate politeness. If a sibling takes advantage of them, show them how to be "kind" in return.

Simplify thoughts and explanations for each age level. Take an active part in sharing and discussing the verses with your children so they learn to meditate on their own level.

Draw the Application

As your children begin to apply the Scriptures they are memorizing to their lives, prompt their creative thinking by asking questions:

What do you think about this verse?

What do you feel about this verse?

How can this verse fit into (apply to) your life?

Open-ended questions, such as these, affirm your children's ideas and inspire creative thinking. This is a good time for you as a parent to add new ideas in the discussion with your children.

Use every opportunity during the week to point out, in a casual manner, how the verses they are learning relate to their lives. Incorporate applications into your prayer time with each child. Ask God to help you be alert to living object lessons. And trust that the Holy Spirit will enlighten your children's minds to the truth of the Word for application to their lives. The Holy Spirit speaks and makes Scripture real to children too.

Do It

It is important for you to help your children relax and enjoy memorization and meditation so they will have a desire to continue the program through their adult years and someday help their children memorize and meditate. As you walk through the steps together, consider these additional helps:

1. Use a five-day schedule. On the weekend give Memorize and Meditate a rest unless an opportune moment occurs for casually teaching the meaning or application of a verse your children are working on.

2. Use incentives. Incentives are not bribery but rewards to reassure your children that their behavior merits value at home. As long as rewards are necessary, feel comfortable about using them to reinforce your values to your children. Make the rewards appropriate for the number of verses your children learn and for their specific ages. The following list gives several suggestions:

AGES 2 TO 5

A sticker	M & M candy	Cookie
Ice cream	Help mom bake	Coloring book
Stay up later	Inexpensive toy	New book
A picnic	Money for whatever	Trip to zoo
First Bible	Shopping trip with mom or dad	

AGES 6 TO 12

Special bike ride	Permission to go to friend's
Lunch with mom and dad	New book or cassette
New clothing item	Slumber party at home
Money for almost whatever	

Attend a major-league game with parents
Toy model—like electric train and accessories

AGES 13 TO 18

New "fad" item	Friend for overnight
Strong's Concordance	Money for almost whatever
New book or cassette	Family car for one day
Item for collection	Leather Bible

Privilege to stay up late one night (at home!)

Dad or mom will do one of their chores
Dinner with dad or mom at an exclusive restaurant

3. Relax with your children. Sit in a comfortable chair or lie on the bed with younger children as they meditate on Scriptures (children six or seven years and older may want to meditate alone). Listen to them talk out loud about the Scriptures they are learning.

4. Keep a positive attitude about Memorize and Meditate. Sometimes children will make mistakes when saying their verses for you. When this happens, repeat the verse in the correct form without drawing attention to the error. This encourages communication and does not dampen their spirits.

There are fifty-two weeks in a year and children attend school for thirteen years, kindergarten through twelfth grade. If a child learns just one verse of Scripture a week for thirteen years, he will learn 676 verses by the time he graduates from high school. With a little more effort, your children can learn the entire book of Mark, which has 678 verses, or they can learn a combination of several passages and chapters:

The Sermon on the Mount	**111 verses**
Ephesians	**155 verses**
Philippians	**104 verses**

1 Timothy	113 verses
James	108 verses
1 John	<u>105 verses</u>
	696 verses

Planting this amount of Scripture in your children's minds will help them develop positive actions and attitudes. If you help and encourage them to memorize and meditate on the Scriptures, and if you are a living example before them, you will, indeed, be "training up" your children in the way they should go.

CHAPTER 1

The Beginning

In the beginning there was God. Then God created the world and all the plants and animals in it. Finally, the Creator looked around and saw that everything was good, but decided to make one more creature. "All these other things are very nice," He may have said. "But I would like to have something in this world to love, something who will love Me." So, He reached down in the dust and made a new creature. The new creature was called "man." And that is how we came to be!

God loves us very much. And He wants us to love Him. But how can we love someone back who we can't see with our eyes? We can't do the things we would do for our other friends. We can't give Him a hug. We can't send Him a birthday present, even if we knew when His birthday is! We can't even bake Him a cake or some chocolate chip cookies. Yet God gives us so much. What can we give Him in return? Jesus, Himself, gave us the answer in the book of Matthew:

You shall love the Lord your God with all your heart, with all your soul, and with all your mind.
Matthew 22:37

When you give God your heart, soul, and mind, you learn more about Him. If God were one of your friends from school, you would want to get to know Him better by spending time with Him.

What does He like? What makes Him happy? What makes Him laugh?

You learn these things from your friends by listening to them and talking with them. You ask them questions. Though you may spend time with them in a group, you also spend time alone with them. It's much easier to get to know someone if there aren't other people around.

"So," you might say, "how can I get to know someone I can't see? I can see my friends and talking with them is so much easier than talking to someone I can't see."

You can get to know God by reading the Bible and understanding what it says. Two ways to do this are by memorizing and meditating on God's Word.

How do you feel about memorizing things? You may be thinking, "I can't memorize anything." But, the fact is, we memorize what we want to remember. You probably can tell me your friends' telephone numbers, or maybe the batting averages of your favorite baseball players. These are things you want to know.

A boy named Matt thought he couldn't spell. He found that when he worked on memorizing the words, he could get 100 percent on his spelling tests. He made flash cards of his words and his mother quizzed him. Sometimes he put the words in stories or sentences. He found a way to use them during class. Doing all these things helped him to go from a "C" in spelling to an "A" in one report card period. It was hard work, but he felt good about himself.

God will give you the power to learn His Word. Ask Him. Just think, if you started to memorize Bible verses in kindergarten and learned one verse each week until you graduated from high school, you would memorize *676 verses!*

When you memorize Scripture, you store in your mind stories and truths about God, His personality, and the way He relates to people. This gives you something to think about and can also help you when you pray to God.

When you think about and talk with God, you are meditating. Most people know what the word *memorize* means, but not everyone knows the meaning of *meditate* or how to do it. Let's see what the word means when it's used in the Bible.

The Old Testament is written in the Hebrew language. Two of the Hebrew words in the Old Testament for *meditate* are *hagah* and *siyach*. *Hagah* (pronounced haw-gaw′) is used in Joshua 1:8: "This Book of the Law shall not depart from your mouth, but you shall meditate in it day and night, that you may observe to do according to all that is written in it." The word *meditate* in this verse means talking quietly with yourself.

The second Hebrew word for *meditate, siyach* (pronounced see-akh), can be found in Psalm 119:15: "I will meditate on Your precepts, and contemplate Your ways." Here, *meditate* means to think about and pray.

In chapters 3—7, you'll learn five D's to help you to learn more about Memorize and Meditate:

Decide How
Determine Where
Discover What
Draw Out Why
Do It

But before you start, there are a few things you need to know.

CHAPTER 2

Before You Start

Before you start to memorize and meditate, you'll need an idea of what's to come and a few tools that will make the rest of the book easier to use. You will learn how to quickly look up Scripture verses in the Bible. And you will learn how to use an index card for meditating.

The Preview

Chapter 3, "Decide How"

In this chapter, I'll give you all the secrets I know about how to memorize. You'll learn about several different ways to memorize. And as you're reading this book, you'll be able to try each of them and use the ones that work best for you.

Chapter 4, "Determine Where"

This chapter will help you choose verses from the Bible to memorize. It contains a checklist with some Bible verses I thought you might enjoy. It gives you some idea of what these verses are about and where to find them. When you finish memorizing your verses for one section, write the date in this book!

Chapter 5, "Discover What"

This chapter may seem to you like some of the work you do at school. (I heard you groaning.

We'll have none of that now. You might even enjoy this.) You'll use a dictionary to discover what the important words in your verse mean. I'll talk about some other steps that you can use to help understand your verse.

Chapter 6, "Draw Out Why"

This is the most exciting part. You'll be looking for ways that your verses fit with your life.

Chapter 7, "Do It"

In this chapter, I'll review what you've learned. There will be a schedule to help you decide how much to memorize each week. And I'll give you some final tools to help you keep your memorization and meditation plan going.

The Cards

I don't mean your birthday cards or your baseball cards! The cards I'm talking about are cards that will help you review the parts of the Bible that you've memorized. If you've ever tried to memorize an oral report for school, you will know that it helps to break your report down into little chunks. The same thing goes for long sections of Scripture.

You will need some 3″ x 5″ index cards and a file box in which to keep them. You can use a different color card for each section of the Bible you

are memorizing, but it is not necessary. Decorate your file box to make it yours. You will be using it for a long time, so make it important to you. You will also need divider cards to separate your index cards into groups of verses. These should have labels so you can write the title of each book/chapter you are studying. Before writing on the index cards, make a label for your book and chapter. In this book I will be using the Beatitudes to help practice the skills we are talking about. (The Beatitudes are words that Jesus gave His disciples during the Sermon on the Mount about the kinds of people that will receive blessings.) You will find these in the fifth chapter of Matthew. So write on your divider label "Matthew 5."

You will need to have your index cards and box before you finish reading this book, because we will do one card together.

The Bible

In chapter 4, I'll talk about some of the different versions of the Bible that you might use. Right now, I'm going to have you look up the Beatitudes we were talking about before. Get your family Bible or the closest one you can find for this exercise.

Open your Bible to the book of Matthew. Yes, that's in the New Testament, which is near the last part of your Bible. Once you have Matthew, look for a large number "5." You may have to turn a few pages before you find it. After you've found the large number "5," look for a little number "3." Congratulations! You have just found Matthew 5:3, the first Beatitude.

You can also use the headings at the top of the page like we did when we looked up the verse in our *Nelson's Children's Bible*. Your Bible page might look like one of the two pictured on the following page.

You will be writing six things on each card:

1) the verse number to help you find it again
2) the verse itself

MATTHEW 5:3   836

3 "Blessed *are* the poor in spirit,
    For theirs is the kingdom of
       heaven.
4 Blessed *are* those who mourn,
    For they shall be comforted.
5 Blessed *are* the meek,
    For they shall inherit the earth.
6 Blessed *are* those who hunger and
       thirst for righteousness,
    For they shall be filled.
7 Blessed *are* the merciful,
    For they shall obtain mercy.
8 Blessed *are* the pure in heart,
    For they shall see God.
9 Blessed *are* the peacemakers,
    For they shall be called sons of
       God.
10 Blessed are those who are
       persecuted for right
          sake.

Murder Be
21 "You
those of
and whoe
of the jud
22 "But I
angry wit
shall be ir
whoever s
be in dang
says, 'You
fire.
23 "There
the
b

chapter

verse

cross reference

The Beatitudes

5 And seeing the mul
   up on a mountain, and wh
seated His disciples came to Him.
2 Then He opened His mouth a
taught them, saying:

3 "Blessed *are* the poor in spirit,
    For theirs is the kingdom of heaven.
4 Blessed *are* those who mourn,
    For they shall be comforted.
5 Blessed *are* the meek,
    For they shall inherit the earth.
6 Blessed *are* those who hunger and
       thirst for righteousness,
    For they shall be filled.

20 "For
righteousn
the scribes
means ente

Murder Beg
21 "You h
those of o
and whoev
the judgme

15 Isaiah 9:1, 2   16 Exodus 20:13; Deuteronomy 5:17

3) key words and their definitions from a Bible dictionary or concordance
4) definitions of key words from a regular dictionary (in case you still need help understanding the word)
5) your thoughts about what this verse is saying or a clever way you used to memorize it
6) quotes from other books (sometimes it helps to read what other people thought your verse meant)

Now get your first index card and write "Matthew 5:3" in the top left-hand corner of the card. Then, copy the verse exactly as it appears in your Bible onto the card.

Don't forget capital letters and punctuation! This will be important when you memorize. If you have trouble writing small enough to fit the verse on your card, ask one of your parents to help.

You've just gone through the first two steps of memorization. Keep your index cards nearby, because you'll be using them as you learn the different methods of memorization and as you begin to meditate on the verses you memorize.

CHAPTER 3

Decide How

"How could I remember all those verses?" "I'm just not good at remembering things." If either of these thoughts popped into your mind, then this chapter is for you. I'm going to give you five different ways to help you remember Bible verses. You can use one or more of these methods when you memorize your own verses. For right now, try each method with Matthew 5:3. Later, when you do your own verses, pick the ones you like the best.

Method #1: REPEAT REPEAT REPEAT

Most people use repetition when they memorize.

There are several steps to this method.

Read the verse several times.

Find Matthew 5:3 in your Bible. You can use your card since you have already written it. Read the verse at least three times so it sticks in your mind like chewing gum. Try to be in a quiet place, so you can think. Your bedroom or a quiet place outdoors is a better choice than a crowded playground or a football game.

Now, *see* the verse in your mind.

Look closely at your verse, then try to picture it. Did you notice the big words? How about the periods? Do you know which words have capital letters? Do that now with Matthew 5:3. Make sure you always use the same Bible from which to memorize so that the picture of that verse will always be the same in your mind.

Talk the verse.

When you are talking out loud, you are using both your voice and your ears. It may seem strange to you at first, but this helps you learn twice as fast. Say the verse out loud. Try whispering it. If you're not in a library, try shouting it. See what works best for you.

Write the verse three times.

You won't need to write out every verse you memorize, but if you're stuck on a verse, this can help. Use a sheet of paper other than your index card to do this. (You can use the space below to write Matthew 5:3.)

Exodus 20:8

Remember the Sabbath day, to
keep it holy.
Remember the Sabbath day, to
keep it holy.
Remember the S

Stretch your mind.

Just as your body needs exercise at recess and P.E., your mind also needs a workout. Start those brain push-ups: 1, 2, 3, 4. You can use this exercise.

Try to remember as much of the verse as you can before checking yourself in the Bible. Try to do a little more each time. By stretching your mind this way, you're doing the same thing for your mind that the push-ups do for your body. You will get more out of it each time you exercise.

Learn every word.

You haven't learned a verse if you haven't learned it perfectly. Take an index card. Place it over the verse. Move it down one line at a time as you say it. Cover what you're saying. Then, uncover it to check. *No peeking!*

Take a recess.

You use recesses at school to put space between subjects that you're learning. Use this for learning Bible verses too. Say your verse three times. Then, take a break. Later, say it three more times. Take another break, and say it again three times. How long a break should you take? It could be just a few minutes like a regular recess, or you could say your verse before school, after school, and before you go to bed for your three study times.

Finish what you start.

To feel good about what you are doing, you'll need to finish the verses you've started. I was one of those kids who got excited about a project and worked hard for a while, but then I lost interest and stuck it away in a drawer. By the time I grew up, I had many drawers of unfinished projects.

One thing that has helped me to finish things now that I'm an adult is to reward myself for finishing a project. My reward might be as simple as calling a friend or reading a favorite book. I give myself bigger rewards when I finish a bigger project, such as when I memorize a whole chapter of the Bible. Maybe you can work out a reward system with your parents. To help you keep track of what you've already memorized, I've included a checklist in chapter 4. You can put the date in the last column when you've memorized one of the Bible sections listed.

Method #2: FORM ACRONYMS

An acronym is made when you take the first letters of a group of words and make a new word. For example, most schools have a P.T.A. This acronym stands for the words *Parent–Teacher Association*. You can use this method for memorizing tough Bible lists too.

Pick out the key words in your verse. I'll use the first of the Beatitudes, Matthew 5:3:

> Blessed are the poor in spirit,
> For theirs is the kingdom of heaven.

The key words are *blessed, poor, spirit, kingdom,* and *heaven*. The acronym would be BPSKH. If memorizing this strange new word isn't enough, you can also create a new sentence using these letters. In the space below, list at least five words you know that begin with "B," "P," "S,"

"K," and "H." Then, choose a word from each list to make a sentence. For instance, Bears Paint Silly Kangaroo Houses.

B	P	S	K	H
Bears	Paint	Silly	Kangaroo	Houses
1.	1.	1.	1.	1.
2.	2.	2.	2.	2.
3.	3.	3.	3.	3.
4.	4.	4.	4.	4.
5.	5.	5.	5.	5.

You can add your favorite sentence from above to the back of your index card.

Method #3: ASSOCIATE

See a silly picture in your mind that goes along with your verse. For instance, you might imagine yourself with a see-through crown on your head or as a poor king or queen dressed in robes with holes in them to help you see in your mind a literal picture of "poor in spirit." Take a minute now to draw what comes into your mind when you think of the words of Matthew 5:3. (Use the space provided.) You can make the picture as silly as possible to help you remember. But if you're spending more time trying to think up a silly picture for your verse than you are memorizing that verse, you probably don't need to use this method.

Association works well with descriptive passages, such as Ephesians 6:10–20, which gives a picture of what it is to "take up the whole armor of God," or Romans 8:31–39, which gives a picture of God's everlasting love. You'll see how much easier it is to remember verses, such as Ephesians 6:14, "Stand therefore, having girded your waist with truth," when you imagine yourself wearing an oversized belt made of the word TRUTH.

Method #4: RECORD ON CASSETTE

If you have a tape recorder, record yourself reading the Beatitudes. Then, play it back over and over again to check yourself. You could record one verse several times or recite a whole section. If you don't want to listen to your own voice, have your parents or one of your friends record the verses for you. If you have a tape recorder, go ahead and try this now. The best time to play the tape back is right before you go to sleep at night. This is when your mind can work best without being distracted by other thoughts.

Method #5: MAKE UP SONGS

Take the words of the verse you are learning and put it to a song you already know. How about singing the Beatitudes to the tune of "Yankee Doodle" or Psalm 24 to "When the Saints Go Marching In"?

If you can't think of a song to fit your verse, make one up. It doesn't have to be a great melody. It just has to help you remember the verse. Teach your song to someone else or put homemade instruments with it to really help the words stick with you. On a bad day this can make you laugh. See if you can sing Matthew 5:3 to the tune of "Yankee Doodle" now. You will probably run out of words before you run out of music, but you can always add the rest of the Beatitudes later.

Now that I've told you all my secrets for memorizing Bible verses, you'll need to find the verses you want to memorize.

1. Blessed are the poor in spir - it

CHAPTER 4

Determine Where

How do you decide what to memorize in the Bible? You can use what I call The Doctor Doolittle Method. Whenever the doctor wanted to begin a voyage, he would get his chart book and a pin. He'd close his eyes, open the book and stick the pin in a page. Wherever the pin stuck, that's where the ship would go.

This method of memorization has two major problems. First, it puts too many holes in an already holy book. Second, picking a place to begin at random is like reading only the middle of a book. You miss what comes before and what comes after your verse.

Another way to memorize is by using what I call the freight train method. This means that you start at Genesis and memorize each verse, straight through to Revelation. Although this allows you always to know what comes before your verse, it has problems too. By using this method, you would be very, very old by the time you got to Jesus in the New Testament.

So how do we find out where to start? Pray to God. He knows what is going on in your life and will guide you to what will help you the most in the Bible. God is there when you make the baseball team. God knows when you've done badly on a test or feel lonely. God's right there beside you when you have a bright idea. He cares for you. He will guide you to what you need to learn. You probably won't hear a voice saying, "Brian, read the Beatitudes." But you might have a Sunday school lesson on them or hear a song about them or have someone ask you if you've read them.

Sometimes God is not that direct. So if you're still not sure what to memorize, choose a story that you've always loved, maybe one of the parables of Jesus. (These are found in the books of Matthew, Mark, Luke, or John.) You could ask your parents to tell you their favorite chapter in the Bible. Don't be afraid to talk to your parents or a friend about what you're doing. God often speaks through people we care about and who love us.

Once you've decided where to start, choose a section of Scripture—several verses from one chapter, not individual verses from several locations. This will help you find the verses you have memorized later. It is easier to find something again the more time you spend with it. Start with a small section of verses. Do not try to memorize a whole book on your first try.

I've listed some verses on the next few pages. If there are too many choices for you, try one of the following passages: Psalm 1, Psalm 23, Matthew 6:9–13, or Luke 10:30–37.

Don't let large sections of verses scare you. Memorize each section one verse at a time. Always try to quote the whole passage along with each new verse you learn. Say verse one; then verses one and two; then verses one, two, and three.

You can use the topics in the chart on pages 49–50 to help you find verses that may relate to what is going on in your life right now. Perhaps you've looked outside recently and wondered why God created the sun, moon, and stars. If so, you'll want to memorize and meditate on the creation story. Or if you're afraid you won't make the baseball team, you may want to read a passage about trusting God.

After you have memorized a particular set of verses, you can write the date of completion in the last column in the chart. I've also included a list of verses for Memorize and Meditate, which is arranged according to age groups, at the back of this book. If you want to find passages that are particularly good for people your age to memorize, you can look there.

Make Your Own Choice

Before you learn how to meditate on Scriptures, see how the methods of memorization that you learned in chapter 3 work when you choose your own verse from one of the lists on pages 49–50 or 89–96. Remember this verse, because you'll be meditating on it later.

BIBLE SECTION CHECKLIST

TOPIC	BIBLE CHAPTER AND VERSE	DATE COMPLETED
The Creation Story	Genesis 1:1—2:4	
The First Rainbow	Genesis 9:8–17	
The Commandments	Exodus 20:1–17 Matthew 22:36–40 John 13:34, 35 Ephesians 6:1–3	
Being Afraid	Deuteronomy 31:6–8 Joshua 1:7–9 Matthew 14:22–33	
Choosing Good or Evil	Deuteronomy 30:11–20 Psalm 1	
Who Is God?	Psalm 19	
The Shepherd Psalm	Psalm 23	
Trusting God	Psalm 37:3–8 Proverbs 3:3–6	
God Is with Us	Psalm 46	
Praising God	Psalm 100 Psalm 150	
The Importance of God's Law	Psalm 119:1–16 Psalm 119:33–48	
God's Help	Psalm 121	
God's Call	Genesis 12:1–4 Exodus 3:1–10 1 Samuel 3:1–10 Acts 26:12–18	
Peace	Isaiah 26:1–4 Isaiah 55:12, 13 Philippians 4:4–9	

TOPIC	BIBLE CHAPTER AND VERSE	DATE COMPLETED
Giving to God	Matthew 6:1–4 2 Corinthians 9:6–8	
The Lord's Prayer	Matthew 6:9–13	
The Beatitudes	Matthew 5:1–12	
Parables: The Talents The Good Samaritan	Matthew 25:14–30 Luke 10:30–37	
Forgiving Others	Ephesians 4:25–32	
The Christmas Story	Luke 2:1–20	
The Easter Story	Luke 24:1–12	
Jesus Called Disciples	Matthew 4:18–22 Mark 3:13–19	
Healing the Blind Man	John 9:1–11	
Feeding the 5,000	John 6:1–21	
The Good News	Romans 10:9, 10 Ephesians 2:8, 9	
Free from Sin	Romans 8:1–11	
Love	1 Corinthians 13	
The Fruit of the Spirit	Galatians 5:22–26	
Armor of God	Ephesians 6:10–20	
The Race	Philippians 3:12–14	
The Tongue	James 3:1–12	
Fellowship with God	1 John 1	

CHAPTER 5

Discover What

Ministers and Sunday school teachers are not the only people who can discover the meaning of Bible verses. You, too, can understand their meaning. Meditation is one way to do this. And, in the rest of this chapter, I will help you learn how to meditate. You can take my ideas and add your own to learn more from God.

You will need some books to help you. The first one is a Bible. I have been using the New King James Version in this book. Many people find it easier to memorize than some other versions. If you already have another version, you can use it or a family Bible.

The second book you need is a concordance or a Bible dictionary. Your family may already have

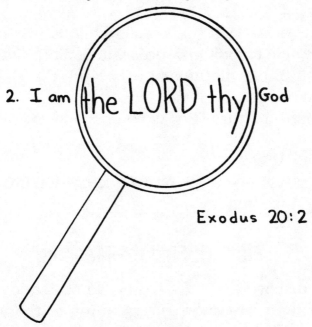

2. I am the LORD thy God

Exodus 20:2

a concordance like the *New Strong's Exhaustive Concordance of the Bible.* I used *Nelson's Illustrated Bible Dictionary* for the verse we are about to look up. A concordance is a book that gives you Bible verses that contain a certain word. This will help you find other places in the Bible that talk about the same thing as the verse or section you are studying. These books are difficult to use by yourself. You may need some help from your parents the first time you use them. Make sure your concordance refers to the version of the Bible you are using. If not, the word you're looking up might not be in there. Sometimes Bibles will have a dictionary, word list, or concordance in the back of the book. Check your Bible to see if it does.

The third book you need is a regular dictionary to be able to look up words you don't understand in the Bible dictionary or would like to know more about.

Again the three books you need for meditation are:

1. **A Bible**
2. **A concordance or a Bible dictionary**
3. **A dictionary**

Step #1: Find the Meaning

In discovering what a Bible verse is about, the first step is to know the meaning of the words.

Only look up the important words. *Of, a, are,* and *you* are nice words, but you probably already know their meaning. Even if you don't, they aren't as important as other words in your verse. You will not have time to research every word. Some verses will have one or two important words. Other verses will have many. Just because a verse has few important words does not mean that you shouldn't study the verse. Sometimes those simple verses can mean the most to you.

Use a Concordance and a Dictionary

You can find the meanings of words from Old Testament passages in the Hebrew dictionary at the back of a concordance and the meanings of words from New Testament passages in the Greek dictionary. When you are looking for the meanings of words in a concordance, first find the word in the front of the book. Then find the particular Scripture verse where the word appears. Next to the reference, you will find a number that refers you to the definition of the word in one of the dictionaries at the back of the book.

Before you look up words in a regular dictionary, find meanings in a Bible dictionary. Let's use our verse, Matthew 5:3, to do this:

Blessed are the poor in spirit,
For theirs is the kingdom of heaven.

I might decide to find the word *blessed* in the Bible dictionary. Looking under "B," just as if I were searching in the dictionary, I would try to find my word. In the *Nelson's Illustrated Bible Dictionary*, which I'm now using, *blessed* is not listed but *bless, blessing* is. As you can see in the close-up of the dictionary page shown below, several definitions are given under the word. Different verses in the Bible that use the word in other ways are included. Here's what the entry for

over the bed-chamber"—of Herod (Acts 12:20).

BLEACHER (see Occupations and Trades).

BLEMISH (see Disabilities and Deformities).

BLESS, BLESSING — the act of declaring, or wishing, God's favor and goodness upon others. The blessing is not only the good effect of words; it also has the power to bring them to pass. In the Bible, important persons blessed those with less power or influence. The patriarchs pronounced benefits upon their children, often near their own deaths (Gen. 49:1-28). Even if spoken by mistake, once a blessing was given it could not be taken back (Genesis 27).

Leaders often blessed people, especially when getting ready to leave them. These included Moses (Deuteronomy 33), Joshua (22:6-7), and Jesus (Luke 24:50). Equals could bless each other by being friendly (Gen. 12:3). One can also bless God, showing gratitude to Him (Deut. 8:10) in songs of praise (Ps. 103:1-2).

God also blesses people by giving life, riches, fruitfulness, or plenty (Gen. 1:22, 28). His greatest blessing is turning us from evil (Acts 3:25-26) and forgiving our sins (Rom. 4:7-8).

Cases of the opposite of blessing, or cursing, are often cited in the Bible (Deut. 27:11-26). Although

185

bless, blessing looks like in my Bible dictionary. Notice all the other Bible verses that are listed in the definition.

Get your index card with Matthew 5:3 again, and write under the verse the definition of *bless:* "The act of declaring or wishing God's favor and goodness upon others." You don't have to write the entire definition; just include enough to help you understand the meaning of the word.

After the definition, write the initials N.I.B.D. for *Nelson's Illustrated Bible Dictionary.* This will remind you where you found your definition, in case you want to look up the word again.

If your Bible dictionary includes other Scripture verses in the definition, you may want to look up these verses to see if they help you understand more about the words you are studying. You'll notice in the definition of *blessed* from my dictionary, *Nelson's Illustrated Bible Dictionary* (Nashville: Thomas Nelson, 1986), that there are several Scripture references. These refer to specific places in the Bible where either the word *bless* is used or where a blessing is being given.

If you still aren't clear about what *blessed* means, use your dictionary. You will need to look up *bless* again, because *blessed* probably won't be in there. Try to find a definition that matches the way the word is used in your verse. Write the definition on your card under the last sentence you wrote. Make sure that you put initials for your dictionary title next to the definition so you can find it again just like you did for the Bible dictionary.

You're doing great! You've just finished the front side of your card. You've done four of the six things that will be written on the card. Look at my card on this page. See if yours looks about the same. I didn't use a regular dictionary for this card, so yours may have more writing. It doesn't have to be exactly the same. But if it's close, you're on the right track.

Matthew 5:3
Blessed are the poor in spirit,   For theirs is the kingdom of heaven.

Bless-(N.I.B.D., p. 185) the act of
    declaring, or wishing God's favor and
    goodness upon others

Also read Matthew 5:10, 5:19 and 25:34

Where Else Can I Look?

If you want to read what someone else thought your verse meant, you could look it up in a book called a commentary. For our verse, you would need a commentary on the book of Matthew. Most families don't have commentaries on every book in the Bible at home. But most ministers do. You can ask your minister, or you can look in your church library. Some writers can be hard to understand, so have someone help you pick one that will be right for you. If you find something in the commentary that helps you understand the verse better, you could write this on the back of your card.

Now try these steps of meditation on the verse you chose after reading chapter 4. If you haven't already done so, write the book of the Bible, chapter number and verse in the upper left-hand corner of an index card. Copy the verse exactly the way it looks in your Bible. Pick out your key words, then look them up and write the definitions on the card. (Use the space below if you want to practice in the book.)

Pay attention to periods, commas, and other punctuation. They can help you understand verses. For instance, if the comma in Matthew 5:3

were after the word *poor* instead of *spirit,* the verse would seem to mean something else. It would sound as if the verse were talking about how much money the person had instead of how much he or she needed God. One other thing, don't skip over verses because you think they're boring. Sometimes these verses can be the most exciting, once they make sense.

Step #2: Ask God for Help

The second step is to ask God for understanding. Sometimes you may think, "What does this verse really mean?" Ask God. He doesn't mind. He wants you to ask. That's how you learn. When you don't understand something in school, what do you do? You ask your teacher, don't you? Well, God is the greatest teacher around. He wrote the textbook—the Bible—remember? Again, God probably won't say, "Now, Maria, Matthew 5:3 means . . ." Being still sometimes helps you discover answers you didn't think you knew. Or, He might bring someone into your life who can help answer your questions. Try asking your parents, or your minister, or a friend you trust.

To understand even more, ask yourself questions about the verse. Think about it. Talk to yourself as you think about the verses. Remember, to meditate means to talk quietly to yourself.

Pretend you're explaining your verse to a friend

or your brother or sister. If you have a pet, try talking to him or her about the verses. Your family may think you've gone crazy, but once they understand what you're doing, I'm sure they'll help. When you were very little, you talked to yourself all the time. It helped you to learn then. It can help you now.

Step #3: Say It Your Way

The third step is putting it in your own words. Put your name in the verse. After you have discovered the meaning of the more difficult words, rewrite the verse in words that are easier to understand. Put your name in the verse to make it more personal. For example, our verse, Matthew 5:3, might come out sounding like this:

Happy are you, Jennifer, because you know when you need God's help, for heaven is with you.

Some people like to do this for every verse they study. It helps them to feel like the Bible was written just for them. If you're one of those people, you could copy this verse in your own words on the back of your Matthew 5:3 card.

Once you've looked up all the words and gone through all the steps, then it's time to sit quietly with God. Sometimes, when we spend time with

God, we do all the talking. Have you ever had a friend that talked all the time, every time you were together? You probably had things you wanted to say, but you couldn't get a word in.

God wants a chance to talk to us, just as you want a chance to talk with your friend. That's why when you meditate, you should be listening more than talking. Think about what you've learned from your verse. Give God a chance to put the pieces of its meaning together for you just like a puzzle. Remember, find a quiet place where you and God can be alone together.

When you are ready to meditate, lie down on your bed. (Go ahead, try it. I dare you.) You can think best when you are comfortable. Make sure

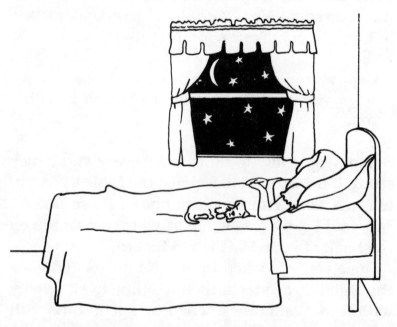

your radio or tape player is off and that the room is quiet. Relax completely. Start by breathing deeply. When you are completely relaxed, begin to think about God and the Bible verse you are memorizing. Think about all those key words you've looked up and what they mean to you. Think about the words you changed to put the verse into words you could understand. It's amazing what you can learn when you are still and quiet with God!

Now that you know how to meditate, you can use this in the next chapter where you can think about what this verse means in your life.

CHAPTER 6

Draw Out Why

Drawing out why the verse we're studying is important in our lives is the hardest skill to practice. Sometimes it is very hard because what God is asking us to do may be different from what we would like to do. One day, my verse for memorizing was Ephesians 4:32: "And be kind to one another, tenderhearted, forgiving one another, just as God in Christ also forgave you." I was very angry at a friend of mine. After I read the verse, I knew that God wanted me to forgive that friend, even though I was mad.

Sometimes you will have a happy verse to memorize like Luke 2:14: "Glory to God in the highest, And on earth peace, good will toward men!" And something good will happen that day that makes you want to shout the verse out loud. The good thing about meditating is that the longer I think about what God wants me to do, I begin to want to do it.

There are three things to remember to make the Bible real for you: Use it every day; speak the verse when you need it; remember that the stories are real.

Use the Bible Every Day

I like to start the day memorizing and meditating on a new Bible verse. I think about how this verse might be important to me. Sometimes I take a walk with God in the morning and think about my verse. I look for signs of the verse in the world around me and in my own life. If you walk to school, you might want to try that, too. If you take the bus, maybe you could take a ride with God. I'm finding out that my day just isn't right without this special morning time. If you think better in the afternoon or evening, those could be your times with God. You could think about what happened that day. How did God speak to you on the playground? In the classroom? At home?

Say the Verses When You Need Them

You may experience some "close calls" in your life. You may come close to having an accident; someone may hurt your feelings; you may feel scared or lonely. You can feel God with you, keeping you safe in these times. You can hear Him talking to you through His Word.

At other times, you may be so full of joy that you want to tell everybody how you feel. Think of your mind as a computer. When you practice memorization and meditation, you are giving your mind input. When you need Him the most, God will help you get the verse from your memory bank that will be just what you need to hear.

When the devil tempted Jesus in the desert, what did Jesus do? Did He stick out His tongue and call the devil names? Did He run away and hide? No, He remembered verses He had memo-

James 2:8~... Thou shalt love thy neighbor as thyself.

rized as a child and used them to help Him through that hard time.

When you are asked to do something wrong you, too, can remember Bible verses, as long as you have taken the time to memorize and meditate on them. If someone asks you to steal something, you might use Exodus 20:15, "You shall not steal," to help you not steal. If your mother said you could stay overnight with your best friend, you might want to "Make a joyful shout to the Lord" (Psalm 100:1).

Remember the Stories Are Real

Try to think of John or Luke as your friend, telling you the story of another friend, Jesus. At Christmastime, memorize and meditate on the Christmas story. At Easter, look to the resurrection story to make that season come alive for you. The reason there are so many names and dates and places that are hard to say in the Bible is that the author of that book wanted you to know that the story was real. The Bible doesn't begin "Once upon a time . . ." like a fairy tale. It also doesn't end "And they lived happily ever after." These were real people who had real-life problems and, with God's help, they made it through.

If you're reading a confusing section, sometimes asking yourself questions as you study can help you learn more. Maybe your parent or friend could make up some questions. For example, as you study the Beatitudes, you may ask yourself, Who was Jesus talking to? What is a Beatitude? Why did Jesus make all of these statements? Which one of the Beatitudes is most like me? Which one would I like to be? What Beatitude might Jesus add if He were saying these today?

Once you've asked these questions, use the books you learned about in chapter 5, or go to someone you think could help you find the answers to your questions. Your parents or minister or Sunday school teacher may be able to help. They may not know the answers to your questions, but God can speak through them to help you find those answers.

Make Jesus your best friend. Tell Him all the things you would tell a friend about what is going on in your life and how much you care for Him. Then, look for His answers both in the Bible and in your life. When you discover some of these answers, you might want to write them on your index card. That way, they're always with you.

Now, you are ready to try this on your own. Let me give you a few more tips to help you begin and continue to memorize and meditate.

CHAPTER 7

Do It

Take a minute to remember the D's you've learned so far in this book:

Decide How
Determine Where
Discover What
Draw Out Why

Now it's time to *Do It*. How? Here are some helps:

1. **Schedule**
2. **Pray**
3. **Relax**
4. **Think Positive**

Schedule

Make time each day for the Bible. Talk to your parents. Find a time of day when you are almost always at home. It is important to set this time aside for God. Sometimes you have to make choices about what is really important. Maybe this could be a time when the whole family studies the Bible. Each person can memorize his own verses of Scripture. You could follow with a family talk time where each person shares what they've learned.

Pray

There are many times you can pray while you're doing it. Pray before you start to help you get still. Be quiet before God. If you work on a verse for a long time and can't seem to make sense of it, pray. Say something like: "God, I know You're trying to tell me something, but I don't know what it is." He won't get mad at you, but He will give you some help. You may not get the answers now but that's all right. God will give you the answers when the time is right.

Relax

You should be enjoying this time with God. If not, something is wrong. Don't push yourself to learn too many verses too fast. If your parents want you to learn more quickly, talk to them about your feelings. This should be a fun time for the whole family. Don't forget about those recess times! Your mind needs a break every once in a while.

Think Positive

Say, "I can." When you say "I can't!" you can't. Here is a Bible verse to memorize that will help you when you're stuck.

I can do all things through Christ who strengthens me.

Philippians 4:13

This doesn't mean we should brag to others about how many Bible verses we've memorized. Friends don't like to hear things like that. They'll "see" the verses by how your life changes as you become the person God wants you to be.

Let me give you a word I'll call "The Big C"— *Consistency*. This means you need to keep memorizing and meditating those verses even when you don't feel like it. Here are three C's to help you:

1. **Carry your cards.**
2. **Continue to review.**
3. **Call on a buddy.**

Carry Your Cards

You should have at least one complete index card by now. On the next page you will see what mine looked like when it was done.

Set Your Goals

Decide each week how many verses you will be able to learn. If you have a busy week, choose only a few verses. If your calendar is blank, choose more verses. If you think your week is free, and then Mom tells you Aunt Ernestine is coming to visit, or the coach calls four extra practices, or your music teacher tells you that you're playing for the Queen of England, don't give up. Just do the verses you missed next week. If all

Happy are you, Jennifer, because you
know when you need God's help,
for heaven is with you.

B - Blessed   Bears
P - poor   Paint
S - spirit   Silly
K - kingdom   Kangaroo
H - heaven   Houses

your weeks become busy, it may be time to sit down with your parents and talk about what is important to you.

Set goals that you can do. Don't try to do twenty verses in one week. Pick a number that you can easily work on and be able to remember. Usually one to three verses are plenty. This is not a race. If your brother or sister is memorizing five verses a week, it doesn't mean you have to memorize five verses. It's more important that you finish the goal you've set for yourself than try to learn the same as or more verses than anyone else.

Keep the verses you are studying someplace where you can see them. How about the refrigerator? If you have a bulletin board in your room, that's a good place too. If you have a younger brother or sister who might pull the cards down, or put sticky candy on them, or color all over them, you may want to put a plastic sandwich bag over them for protection. Once you've memorized that section, put your cards in your file box, so you can review them at another time.

Imagine yourself traveling from Seattle to Boston. This trip is about 3,000 miles. At first, that sounds like a lot, but when you break down the distance into what you will travel each day, it looks easier. Think of the goals you set each week like the towns that you will stay in each night of your trip. As you come to each town, you will be closer to finishing your journey. As you finish

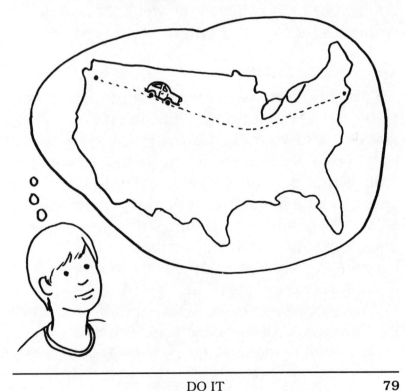

each goal, you are getting closer to the end of your trip. Before you know it, you've reached the end, memorizing the verses you have chosen from the Bible. You can enter the date you complete the verses in your "trip" in chapter 4.

If you need to break your trip down even further, use the schedule on page 81 to help you memorize and meditate each week for as little as fifteen minutes a day.

Remember, you don't have to follow this schedule exactly. Find what works for you. Just make sure that you give yourself time to listen to God, write out the cards, and review. This schedule could start on any day of the week. Choose what works best for your family.

Use a Card Holder

Carrying your cards with you can give you some extra practice time. This doesn't mean you need to carry your file box wherever you go. Take only the cards you're working on and maybe the rest of that section for review. Find something you already have that will hold those cards. Maybe you have a billfold, small purse, or a pocket calendar that the cards could fit in. You could make a holder out of an envelope or a sheet of construction paper.

Why carry your cards with you? If you're sitting around waiting to be picked up, they're a good way to make use of your time. If you have a

SUGGESTED WEEKLY GUIDE

1st Day—15 minutes
1. Start with prayer.
2. Write out one card.
3. Memorize first verse.
4. Read notes in your Bible for that verse.

2nd Day—15 minutes
1. Start with prayer.
2. Review yesterday's verse.
3. Look up unknown words.
4. Write what the verse means to your life.

3rd Day—15 minutes
1. Start with prayer.
2. Write out card for second verse.
3. Memorize second verse.
4. Read notes in your Bible for that verse.

4th Day—15 minutes
1. Start with prayer.
2. Review second verse.
3. Look up unknown words.
4. Write what the verse means to your life.

5th Day—15 minutes
1. Start with prayer.
2. If your goal was two verses, review the verses you learned and add them to your cards as needed. If your goal was three verses, write out the card for the next verse.

6th and 7th Days—
Rest and review the verses you've learned this week.

friend who's also memorizing and meditating, you could share your cards. Sometimes if you've had a really bad day, rereading your cards is like feeling God right there beside you.

Continue in Review

Make sure when you finish a section that you don't forget all about it. Go back and review once in a while. Think back to your trip. Reviewing a section you've already memorized is like looking at your pictures after you've come back from a vacation. It's reliving the trip all over again.

How often should you review? That depends on you—your schedule and how well you remember things. Perhaps your family could set aside a once-a-month or twice-a-month review session. Everyone in the family could review their cards and then share what they've learned.

Call on Your Buddy

Choose one person in your family or a close friend to be your study buddy. This should be someone you are able to talk to at least once a week. Make sure that the person you choose will get excited when you've reached your goal. Ask your buddy to hold your cards for the week and listen to you say your verses. Then you can do the same thing for your buddy. If you've just finished

a section of the Bible, see if you can quote the whole section. You might also spend your time sharing anything that you've learned about your verses this week that was especially important to you. Make sure you give your buddy a chance to share too.

Be careful to set aside this time to talk only about the Bible and your verses. Don't get sidetracked into telling your problems this week at school or talking about the new kid that just moved in. This can waste very special time together.

After you have recited your verses, tell each other the corrections you need to make. Be kind. Tell your buddy in a positive way the changes that need to be made.

Remember, you are not in a race with your buddy. Don't be upset if your buddy has more verses to say than you do. You're each taking your own trip. Go at your own pace.

Be faithful to your buddy. Don't say you can't meet with him/her unless it is an emergency. If this is the case, set up another time when you can meet as soon as possible.

Finally, pray for each other. Memorizing and meditating is not easy. Having a buddy will help you reach the end of your trip. If you're able, pray during your time together.

All of these three C's are for one purpose, The Big "C": *Consistency*. They are to help you successfully continue your learning.

One day on a beach in Hawaii, I saw a father teaching his son to surf. The father guided the back of his son's surfboard as he bent down and spoke instructions right into his son's ear. He showed the boy how to watch for just the right waves and told him exactly when to stand up.

As the waves rose James, the son, got into position and began to paddle. He waved at his dad, grinned, and stood up. But the boy fell. Just as he was going under, his dad was right there. He reached down into the waves and carefully placed the boy back onto the surfboard. Then, he told his son to listen again so he could learn to balance. He listened carefully to his father. Soon he was successful at surfing.

When you memorize and meditate, you can hear your heavenly Father give you instructions for your life. He will tell you what to do. If you listen to your heavenly Father, He will help you not to make mistakes. When you fall and get hurt, your Father will be there to rescue you. God will help you get over disappointments. And He will teach you about Himself.

Remember the acronym from page 38? Let's use those letters "B," "P," "S," "K," and "H" to make a new sentence to encourage you to be consistent with Memorize and Meditate:

Buddies Practicing Scriptures Know Him.

Have fun getting to know God!

APPENDIX

Suggested Scriptures
for Memorize and Meditate

You can choose Scriptures from the following lists that are especially good for your age group.

AGES 2 TO 5

The First Rainbow	Genesis 9:8–17
The Ten Commandments	Exodus 20:1–17 Ephesians 6:1–3
The Greatest Commandment	Deuteronomy 6:1–9
Choosing Good over Evil	Joshua 24:14–18
God's Call	1 Samuel 3:1–10
The Good and the Bad	Psalm 1
The Shepherd Psalm	Psalm 23
Praising God	Psalms 100; 150
God's Help	Psalm 121
Giving to God	Malachi 3:8–12
The Beatitudes	Matthew 5:1–12
The Lord's Prayer	Matthew 6:9–13
The Birth of Christ	Luke 2:1–20
The Resurrection	Luke 24:1–12
The New Birth	Romans 10:9–10 Ephesians 2:8–9
Walking in the Spirit	Galatians 5:22–26
Forgiving Others	Ephesians 4:25–32
Armor of God	Ephesians 6:10–20
Right Thinking	Philippians 4:4–9

AGES 6 TO 12

History of Creation	Genesis 1—2
The First Rainbow	Genesis 9:8–17
God's Call	Genesis 12:1–4 Exodus 3:1–10 1 Samuel 3:1–10 Acts 26:12–18
The Ten Commandments	Exodus 20:1–17 Matthew 22:36–40 John 13:34–35 Ephesians 6:1–3
The Greatest Commandment	Deuteronomy 6:1–9
Choosing Good over Evil	Deuteronomy 30:11–20 Joshua 24:14–18
Encouragement	Deuteronomy 31:6–8 Isaiah 41:8–13 Matthew 14:22–33
Success	Joshua 1:7–9 Psalm 1
Obedience	1 Samuel 15:22–23 Matthew 7:21–23
The Good and the Bad	Psalm 1
Who Is God?	Psalm 19
The Shepherd Psalm	Psalm 23
Trusting God	Psalms 37:3–8; 118:5–9 Proverbs 3:3–6
Security in God	Psalm 46
Praising God	Psalms 100; 150
The Excellent Word of God	Psalm 119:1–16, 33–48

God's Help	Psalm 121
Sowing and Reaping	Psalm 126:4–6 Luke 8:4–18 Galatians 6:6–10
Peace	Isaiah 26:1–4; 55:11–13 Philippians 4:4–9
Daniel's Obedience to God	Daniel 1:6–21
Giving to God	Malachi 3:8–12 Matthew 6:1–4 2 Corinthians 9:6–8
Jesus Called Disciples	Matthew 4:18–22 Mark 3:13–19 Luke 5:1–11
The Beatitudes	Matthew 5:1–12
The Lord's Prayer	Matthew 6:9–13
Parables: The Talents The Good Samaritan	Matthew 25:14–30 Luke 10:30–37
Forgiving Others	Mark 11:25–26 Luke 17:1–4 Ephesians 4:25–32
The Birth of Jesus	Luke 2:1–20
The Resurrection	Luke 24:1–12
Miracle of Jesus	John 6:1–21
Healing Miracle of Jesus	John 9:1–11
Free from Sin	Romans 8:1–11
The New Birth	Romans 10:9–10 Ephesians 2:8–9
Love	1 Corinthians 13
Walking in the Spirit	Galatians 5:22–26
Armor of God	Ephesians 6:10–20
Right Thinking	Philippians 4:4–9

| The Tongue | James 3:1–12 |
| Fellowship with God | 1 John 1 |

AGES 13 TO 18

History of Creation	Genesis 1—2
The Fall of Man	Genesis 3
Noah, the Ark, the Flood	Genesis 6—8
The First Rainbow	Genesis 9:8–17
God's Call	Genesis 12:1–4 Exodus 3:1–10 1 Samuel 3:1–10 Acts 26:12–18
The Ten Commandments	Exodus 20:1–17 Matthew 22:36–40 John 13:34–35 Ephesians 6:1–3
The Greatest Commandment	Deuteronomy 6:1–9
Choosing Good over Evil	Deuteronomy 30:11–20 Joshua 24:14–18
Encouragement	Deuteronomy 31:6–8 Isaiah 41:8–13 Matthew 14:22–32
Success	Joshua 1:7–9 Psalm 1
The Walls of Jericho	Joshua 6
Obedience	1 Samuel 15:22–23 Matthew 7:21–23
David and Goliath	1 Samuel 17:32–50
The Good and the Bad	Psalm 1

Giving to God	Malachi 3:8–12
	Matthew 6:1–4
	2 Corinthians 9:6–8
Jesus Called Disciples	Matthew 4:18–22
	Mark 3:13–19
	Luke 5:1–11
The Sermon on the Mount	Matthew 5—7
The Lord's Prayer	Matthew 6:9–13
	John 17
Parables: The Tares,	Matthew 13:24–30,
The Sheep and Goats,	36–43; 25:31–46
The Sower	Luke 8:4–18
Parables: The Treasure,	Matthew 13:44;
The Pearl,	13:45–46
The Sheep,	Luke 15:4–7;
The Coin,	15:8–10;
The Son	15:11–32
The Day of the Lord	Matthew 24:36–44
	1 Thessalonians
	4:13—5:11
Parables: The Talents	Matthew 25:14–30;
The Good Samaritan	Luke 10:30–37
Healing Miracles of Jesus	Mark 5:21–43
	Luke 5:17–25
	John 2:1–12
	John 9:1–11
Discipleship	Mark 8:34–38
	Luke 14:26–33
	John 8:31–36;
	15:1–8
Prayer of Faith	Mark 11:22–26
	John 12: 12–13
	James 1:2–8;
	5:13–18

Forgiving Others	Mark 11:25–26 Luke 17:1–4 Ephesians 4:25–32
The Birth and Resurrection of Christ	Luke 2:1–20 Luke 24
Miracles of Jesus	John 2:1–12 John 6:1–21
The New Birth	John 3:1–21 Romans 10:1–17 Ephesians 2:1–10
The Good Shepherd	John 10:1–15, 22–30
Death and Resurrection of Lazarus	John 11:1–44
Peace	John 14
Abiding in Christ	John 15:1–17
The Holy Spirit	Acts 1:4–8; 2:1–13
Justified by Faith	Romans 4
Christ's Love	Romans 5
Free from Sin	Romans 8
Spiritual Gifts	Romans 12
Freedom in Christ	Romans 14
Gifts and Diversities	1 Corinthians 12
Love	1 Corinthians 13
Walking in the Spirit	Galatians 5:16–26
Walk in Love, Light, and Wisdom	Ephesians 5:1–21
Armor of God	Ephesians 6:1–20
Humility	Philippians 2:1–24
Right Thinking	Philippians 4
Youth in Ministry	1 Timothy 4

Matthew 5:8
    Blessed are the pure in heart,
        For they shall see God.

Matthew 5:9
    Blessed are the peacemakers,
        For they shall be called sons of God.

Matthew 5:10
    Blessed are those who are persecuted for righteousness'
    sake,
        For theirs is the kingdom of heaven.

Matthew 5:11

Blessed are you when they revile and persecute you, and say all kinds of evil against you falsely for My sake.

Matthew 5:12

Rejoice and be exceedingly glad, for great is your reward in heaven, for so they persecuted the prophets who were before you.

Matthew 5:13

You are the salt of the earth; but if the salt loses its flavor, how shall it be seasoned? It is then good for nothing but to be thrown out and trampled under foot by men.